# THE RENAISSANCE CITY

## PLANNING AND CITIES
*(titles published to date)*

# PLANNING AND CITIES

General Editor

GEORGE R. COLLINS, Columbia University

# THE RENAISSANCE CITY

## GIULIO C. ARGAN

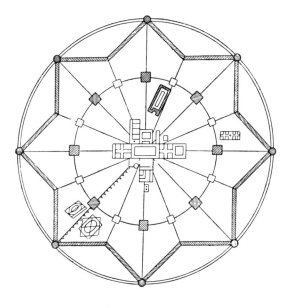

GEORGE BRAZILLER   NEW YORK

Translated by Susan Edna Bassnett

For information address the publisher:
George Braziller Inc.    One Park Avenue    New York, N.Y. 10016
Library of Congress Catalog Card Number: 70–90409
Book design by Jennie Bush
Jacket design by Toshihiro Katayama
Printed  in the Netherlands
Fourth Printing, 1989

# CONTENTS

# GENERAL EDITOR'S PREFACE

During the Renaissance the profession of architect-planner began to develop in Italy. This is evident both from the reshaping of many existing towns and cities and from the ideal conceptualizations of urban form that appeared in architectural treatises of the day. Giulio C. Argan traces the emergence of these attitudes in Italy in the fifteenth and sixteenth centuries, indicating how city planning of the Renaissance correlates with architectural design of the period in general. He stresses the intentional urbanistic character of individual monuments of architecture which we usually study for themselves as separate works of art.

This volume forms part of a series of books on cities and planning. It is our intention to deal with a number of epochs, areas, theoretical positions, and individual planners. While the emphasis is on the physical condition or design of towns and cities, we have tried to enlist authors who are concerned with the social, economic, and political forces that are essential to any understanding of architectural and urban form.

It is our hope that a series of concise, illustrated volumes on various aspects of cities and planning will, by the very different attitudes and assumptions of our several authors, fulfill a need and provide a complement to the more encyclopedic survey books that exist in various languages on the history of architectural city planning.

G.R.C.

# PREFACE

In this brief treatment I am concerned only with those urbanistic factors which in Italy, during the fifteenth and sixteenth centuries, brought about a transformation of the medieval city and tended to establish urban space of a new structure and shape and also a new conception of the historical and political values of the city. I have, therefore, omitted from consideration those changes in European cities, especially in the second half of the sixteenth century, brought about simply by new demographic, economic, and social conditions—circumstances whose influence on the aesthetic configuration of the city would only be felt in the following two centuries. I have also omitted any description of the early phases of colonial urbanization, which would only have important developments on the aesthetic level in the seventeenth century. I have given brief notes in the Appendix on the principal urbanistic changes of European cities, including those outside Italy, which have some artistic interest. These notes are arranged in alphabetical order, by city.

I should like to thank all those who have so kindly helped me in my research for the text and for the illustrative material: Dr. Paola Frandini, Dr. Marcello Fagiolo Dell'Arco, Col. Sergio Longo, to whom I am extremely grateful for the information on systems of fortification, Prof. Giovanni Paccagnini, Prof. Ugo Procacci, and Prof. Bruno Zevi, who have supplied photographs of Sabbioneta, Florence, and Ferrara.

G.C.A.

# INTRODUCTION

Lewis Mumford was correct when he stated in *The City in History* that the Renaissance city does not exist, or rather that in the fifteenth and sixteenth centuries there were no cities which may be called Renaissance in the same way that Siena may be classed as Medieval or Rome as Baroque. Recently, the idea of Renaissance has been given a broader and looser interpretation than in the past, when the Renaissance was defined as a cultural movement based on a new appreciation of the thought and the art of classical antiquity and which, beginning in Italy, afterward spread throughout Europe. The *renovatio* of classical culture, as we now see it, was merely one facet of the vast and complex process of cultural, social, and religious transformations which were coming about in Europe during the fifteenth and sixteenth centuries. More precisely, it was part of the formation of a humanistic culture that radically renewed the very foundations of knowledge and of life through a new conception of the essential values of nature and history.

This humanistic culture was the first to take a conscientious view of the city as the heart of an organized society and as the visible expression of the functions of that society. It was, in fact, the first time since the decline of the classical world—with the rise of this new humanistic culture—that a theory, or science, of the city was created. As we know from our own recent experience, however, the existence of a theory or science of city planning is not enough in itself to transform radically and immediately the realities of the urban phenomenon. It did, nevertheless, constitute a force that influenced more or less effectively the urban transformation brought about by social, economic, and political needs. During the fifteenth and sixteenth centuries, particularly in Italy, the city underwent profound changes that unquestionably laid the basis for the "modern" shape imposed on the great European cities of the seventeenth century. The present study is not intended as a history of the city as a phenomenon during the period known as the Renaissance, but as a history of those urbanistic ideas which contributed to the city's development, whether those ideas were expressed in the writings of theoreticians or in the works of architects.

# THE TRANSFORMATION OF THE CITY

Throughout Europe of the thirteenth and fourteenth centuries, the city was the center of a busy, middle-class community of craftsmen and merchants. The political destiny of the city was decided elsewhere, and city politics consisted only of administrative functions of a commercial nature. Because the city lacked a wide range of political activity, its military apparatus was generally reduced to the defensive circle of its walls. The city appeared as a closely packed aggregation of houses and craftsmen's shops situated around an area of common interest, where the cathedral and the municipal palace were to be found, and where markets and fairs were held (*Fig. 1*). The streets were usually narrow and crooked (*Fig. 2*), with a concentric or radiocentric pattern. The districts and quarters were distinguished by the type of goods produced by their guilds. Since the life of the city was troubled by frequent clashes between factions or families aspiring to greater power, the houses of the chief citizens were fortified, with their towers rising above the common level (*Fig. 3*).

By the end of the sixteenth century the city had acquired a totally different order and appearance: It was viewed as an effective political entity, an active element in a system of conflicting forces rather than as a mere socio-economic organism. A fairly sharp distinction can be observed between the zone of governance and signorial residences—where the control of business was exercised—and the zone of productive activity. The distinction between the main streets where control of public affairs was concentrated, and the secondary streets was also quite clear. There was an increase in the grandeur and number of public buildings, and it was obvious that a political authority stood above the authority of communal administration. In its visible form the city no longer expressed the ideals and interests of a civic community, but rather the values or principles which were based on and justified by its political power. The military apparatus was no longer merely for defense; the city was a nucleus of power in a wider system that comprised a more complex range of interests.

This transformation of the city from a social and economic organism into a political one depended on various factors. The old urban middle class, made up of craftsmen and merchants split; a new elite was formed which assumed control over the cultural and political life of the city and was generally led by a single family or person who held supreme power and decided on war or peace. Often several neighboring cities were under the same power; in this way the line between the dominating and subject cities was drawn, and later became the basis for a system of a capital with provincial centers.

Corresponding to the split in the urban middle class was a new hierarchical order of cultural activities—the distinction between the liberal arts and the mechanical arts. Those activities which involved philosophical premises and historical knowledge could be termed liberal, while the manual activities, presupposing technical and practical skills, could be termed mechanical. The former served a directive purpose; the latter served the resulting, subsidiary purpose of execution. In this way the first separation between the class which conceived plans and the class which carried them out was defined within the social body; this distinction was reflected profoundly in the way in which different techniques or activities were conceived. A sharp differentiation thus came about between ideative techniques—activities of thinking and translation into precise projects—and the work of execution whose sole task was to put such plans into effect was so determined. The consequences of this division for the foundation of a science of city planning were both immediate and important. It became possible to conceive of an project an entire city as a unit without taking account of any difficulties: the financial means, the technical possibilities, the availability of skilled labor. Treatises on architecture in the fifteenth and sixteenth centuries were full of ideal cities, that is, of cities planned *ex novo*, based on purely rational or geometrical criteria.

The distinction between the liberal and mechanical arts led to a division even within the category of working artists; the craftsman was downgraded to workman, while the elite of the old artisan class formed a new class of *artists* and became part of the managerial class, working in direct contact with the *signore* or prince. The most cultured and influential among the artists and those closest to the center of political power were the architects. The ideal city was, in fact, an artistic and political invention of its time, since it was founded on the principle that the perfect architectural and urban form of the city corresponded to the perfection of its political and social arrangements, conceived and

14

carried out by the wisdom of the prince in the same way that the geometry of the plan and the beauty of the buildings were conceived and carried out by the skill of the architect.

The basis of humanist culture was the conviction that God was not so much the beginning as the end of human power and knowledge. Power and knowledge, although no longer attributed to revelation but nevertheless aimed at a consciousness of the divine, had their origin in man, that is to say in reason and in history. This essentially secular, middle-class urban culture lay at the roots of the humanist concept of the city.

The great innovation in the process of urban development was that, beginning in the fifteenth and sixteenth centuries, structural changes in the city were brought about by the will of the prince and the carefully studied plans of architects. Even if the founding of new cities was a rare event, and for the most part determined by precise military or political reasons, the transformation of medieval cities usually occurred in one of the following ways: 1) revision of the old city layout by opening up new streets and wide, regular squares; 2) addition of new sections to the city; and 3) creation of new generative elements through the construction of monumental buildings that were to affect further development of structures in adjacent areas.

# SOURCES: TREATISES

Most architectural treatises on the Renaissance were in agreement during the period of creation and the dissimination of the doctrine of the city. This literature, at once historical and conceptual, first occurred in Italy in the second half of the fifteenth century and was further developed in the sixteenth century, when it spread throughout Europe in translations, adaptations and further treatises. The ultimate source was always the manuscript of Vitruvius; already known and often quoted in the Middle Ages, it became the basic text on which all architectural writings were based after Leon Battista Alberti's monumental work. The first Italian translation, with splendid illustrations and a full commentary, was edited by Cesare Cesariano (Como, 1521) (*Fig. 4*); it was followed by the translation of Francesco Lucio from Castel Durante (Venice, 1524), G. B. Caporali (Perugia, 1526), and, of special importance, the translation by Daniele Barbaro, patriarch of Aquileia (Venice, 1556).

In all Italian architectural discourses, beginning with Leon Battista Alberti's *De re aedificatoria*, written in Rome between 1443 and 1452 with the idealistic aim of seeing the rebirth of the ancient city, the single building was always conceived as an element in a natural or urban context: that is, it is always part of a much larger composition, which is in turn subordinate to norms of symmetry, perspective, and proportion. A more direct interest in city planning can be seen in the treatise by Filarete, written between 1451 and 1464 in Milan and conceived as a series of discussions between the architect and the *signore*, Francesco Sforza (1401–1466). In this tract there is a detailed description of an ideal city: Sforzinda (*Fig. 5*). The perimeter of the city was shaped like an octagonal star, and within the plan there was a carefully drawn distinction between the administrative areas, such as the prince's palace, the cathedral and so on, and the functional ones such as warehouses, shops, and the like. In the treatise by Francesco di Giorgio Martini, written after 1482 at the court of Urbino, there were various plans for cities in which special attention seems to have been given to the relationship between internal arrangement and the fortified city wall (Francesco di Giorgio was a specialist in fortifications). (*Figs. 6–9*).

In the writings of the sixteenth century there was considerably less theorizing about the unitary form of the city. Instead, a whole series of problems involving the reform and development of towns were dealt with directly. Sebastiano Serlio, Andrea Palladio, and Vincenzo Scamozzi were all concerned with the problems of types of buildings, with the need for their forms to correspond to their functions, with the conformity of the building to its natural urban site, and with techniques of construction. The question of a typology was developed in Vignola's *Regole delli Cinque Ordini d'Architettura* (Rules of the Five Orders of Architecture, 1562) with reference to the elements of composition (the classical orders) rather than to the different programs and functions of the buildings. This establishment of a morphology, almost a lexicon or a grammar of building, also hastened the process of subordinating the problem of architecture to that of city planning. The plastic, monumental unity of the building took second place to the new interest in setting up a repertory of forms, which could be described as standardized and which could be combined in various ways to create a continuous, articulate thread with almost no limits as to space and fixed proportional relationships. Twenty years after the publication of Vignola's *Rules*, Domenico Fontana drew up his plan of urban reform for Rome, depriving buildings of every feature of artistic individuality and subjecting them to a street plan, using the classical forms of the now widespread repertory as mere signs of urban "decorum."

Outside Italy, the first great theorist of the city was the greatest German artist of the Renaissance, Albrecht Dürer (1471–1528). His *Unterrichtung zur Befestigung, Schlösser und Flecken* (Discourse on Fortifications, Palaces, and Villages) (Nuremberg, 1527) contained a plan for a square-shaped ideal city (*Fig. 10*). This plan seems to have been the inspiration for Heinrich Schickardt eighty years later, when planning the new city of Freudenstadt, destined to shelter Protestant refugees during the religious wars (*Fig. 11*). The most important German treatise was that of Daniel Speckle, which was reprinted several times between the end of the sixteenth century and the first half of the seventeenth century (*Fig. 12*). It derived from the Italian literature and had a notable influence, albeit much later, on the layout of new cities such as Mannheim, Mülheim, and Karlsruhe in Germany.

# CULTURAL FACTORS

The cultural factors which combined to determine the Renaissance concept of city planning may be grouped as follows: 1) political-military, 2) doctrinal and theoretical, 3) historical-artistic, and 4) practical.

## POLITICAL-MILITARY

This factor had particular influence on the perimeter of the city insofar as it was circled with defensive structures, on the relationship between the city and its surrounding territory, and on the architecture of public and private buildings.

Architectural writings of the Renaissance may be divided into two categories: those dealing with military architecture (which comprised both urban and rural defenses, the setting up of military camps, and the equipment of war in general) and those dealing with civic architecture (which also included religious buildings). But there was no hierarchy of aesthetic values between the two categories, and in the fifteenth century the same architects who constructed churches and palaces in a city frequently built the ramparts around it. Even a pure Platonist like Michelangelo had studied plans of fortifications. In the Renaissance architectural form was conceived of as being an expression and symbol of ideological values. Just as churches should represent a sense of the divine on which the human community was founded, and just as palaces should represent the historical and economic foundation of the city, so the fortifications should represent the ethical-political idea of the security and strength which ensured the freedom of the citizens. The city wall enclosed the main body of the city in the same way a suit of armour enclosed the body of a soldier. A material protection and at the same time a psychological defense, it was meant to arouse fear in the enemy by its terrible aspect and give the combatant a sense of security so that he could both defend himself and strike as well (*Figs. 13–15*). In the Middle Ages fortifications were essentially defensive; in the Renaissance they were both defensive and aggressive.

Moreover, both the political and strategic conditions of military actions had changed. During the fifteenth and sixteenth centuries the rapid development of firearms and the uses to which they could be put had a profound influence on the shape of fortifications. Battles were now conducted from a distance—and no longer under the city walls—so that the first condition of a system of fortification was to make the city difficult to attack while allowing the defenders to hurl crossfire on the surrounding area. The perimeter of the ideal city, usually polygonal and star shaped, came about in order to create salients and reentrants which would enable the defenders to repel with close crossfire any troops which had succeeded in getting below the walls in order to break through the city gates. As it was soon realized that the destructive force of a bullet depended on its angle of impact, the fortifications were required to provide sloping planes against enemy fire, so as to reduce the force of the projectile. Battlements and towers, by now out of date, were abolished because they were an easy target for artillery. Walls were made lower so as to be able to bring up batteries of heavy fire pieces. Fortifications assumed a depth and a striking massiveness, frequently consisting of a ring of walls, prominent jutting ramparts, and the further protection of outworks, moats, and glacis. The system grew more complex, requiring a special science and technology, and became the work of military engineers. From the volumetric point of view, the city walls appeared as a massive composite construction with sharply contrasting projections and recessions which had sloping surfaces and sharp, acute corners (*Figs. 16–18*).

What contributed to making the city wall a true and proper instrument of war, rather than merely a protective circle, was the fact that the city was now part of a much wider political system. Consequently, many minor cities served as defensive outposts around the capital of the state. Sometimes humble villages situated at important strategic points were fortified, thereby acquiring the appearance and status of a city. Toward the end of the sixteenth century new cities were founded for no other purpose than to house military garrisons on frontiers threatened by attack: Such was the case of Palmanova, on the northeast border of the Venetian Republic (*Figs. 80–81*), and of several cities along the Franco-Imperial border such as Hesdin (*Fig. 93*), Philippeville (*Fig. 104*), and Vitry-le-François (see Appendix). Nor is it to be wondered that in these military cities, created to fulfill a precise, practical function, the utopian plan of the ideal city was clearly displayed. These cities were in fact purely instrumental, without a proper society, and therefore not subject to the usual limitations imposed on city-planning reforms by tradition and by the desire to conserve monuments of the city's past.

The study of fortification as a wide-ranging defense implied a new interpretation of the relationship between the city in its enclosed form or volumetric unity and the surrounding territory. In the fourteenth century the surrounding lands or countryside (*contado*) were considered the natural complement of the city's economy and social life. This can be seen clearly in Ambrogio Lorenzetti's fresco, *Good Government*, where the city is presented in architectural and geometric volumes in contrast to the countryside with its delicately undulating lines (*Fig. 3*). The city walls are like a diaphragm through which the peasants must pass to go into the city when taking their produce to market, and the townspeople must pass to go out hunting or to their villas.

From the fifteenth century the relationship became tighter. The circle of walls and ramparts was firmly rooted in the earth, making use of its different levels, its folds, its rises, and its crevices—as in the series of fortified cities in Montefeltro by Francesco di Giorgio Martini (*Figs. 13–15*), in the sixteenth-century fortifications by the Sangallos (*Fig. 16*), and in Michelangelo's famous plan for the fortress of San Miniato al Monte at Florence (*Figs. 17–18*). This new interpretation of the relationship between the city and the surrounding region emerged from the writings of theoreticians of fortifications. In the treatise *Della fortificazione della città* (Venice, 1564), Girolamo Maggi not only studied the form of the perimeter of the walls in relation to the new battle tactics, but stated that the internal structure of the city should be considered in the light of its defensive function (for example, only a few narrow roads should link the city center to the walls). In *Quattro libri di Architettura* (Venice, 1554) by the Sienese Pietro Cattaneo, the shape of the walls and, in particular, the distance between the curtain wall and the bastions, were studied with reference to the maximum range of the artillery. This problem was studied in even greater detail in the treatise *Dell'Architettura militare* (Brescia, 1599) by Francesco de Marchi who insisted on the defensive effectiveness of the *scissors* solution which, naturally, intensified the contrast between planes and the movement of plastic volumes in the light of open space.

The strong volumetric complexes of fortified city walls served also as a point of contact between the natural and the urban landscape. Behind the strong architecture of the walls the main features of the delicate architecture of the city center could be seen emerging (*Fig. 38*). The city on the whole resembled an armored coffer full of precious objects. The two themes, the strong and the delicate, could also be combined and woven together in the same context, as in the facade of the Palazzo Ducale of Urbino, where a row of delicate loggias flanked by finely ornamented windows rise over a steep slope, between two towers topped with parapets (*Figs. 19–20*). This same combination was used even more markedly in the Arch of Alfonso of Aragon in Naples (*Fig. 21*).

## DOCTRINAL AND THEORETICAL

These factors depended essentially on the revival and interpretation of classical Vitruvian theory; from this derived actually the concepts of symmetry and proportion. Although these concepts referred originally to the architectural composition of single buildings they could be extended easily to a cluster of different buildings in a unified context and to the harmony of all those parts which made up the total effect of the city. Starting with the idea of a unitary space of geometrical structure in which all the values were in proportion to each other, it was impossible not to see the need for a proportional relationship between the buildings situated in that space. Since the geometrical structure of space is *perspective*, a proportional composition is also a perspective composition. The novelty in the Renaissance concept of space lay in the fact that perspective was no longer considered as the law of our vision but as the constructive rule of space itself; consequently, it was important as a principle of distribution of buildings in the design of the city. A typical example of the layout of a city which observed the principles of symmetry, perspective, and proportion was Pienza, completed by Bernardo Rossellino for Pius II Piccolomini about 1460 (*Figs. 22–24*).

These principles had a profound influence on the design and modification of the layout of streets and squares in that both had a perspective made up of parallel and orthogonal lines (*Figs. 25–26*). In this way there came about the need for urban vistas, which continued to be of fundamental importance even after the Renaissance. The relationship between city planning and stage design, which was to become so important in the baroque period, can already be sensed. The concept of the city as the stage for human actions was related to the new social structure. Movements in politics are historical movements, and the city, therefore, was the historical center of historical actions. A qualitative difference separated the historical actions of the urban community from the nonhistorical, purely naturalistic activities of rural communities. Also, within the urban community there were distinct class divisions: There were the principal figures, the powers behind city politics, who directed affairs but did not work and there were the people who worked but did not direct. The center of the city was the typical setting for the actions of great men, the historic background for historic figures (*Figs. 27–28*).

## HISTORICAL-ARTISTIC

This factor was complex. What gave cohesion to the urban community was no longer a common interest in economic prosperity, but the thought of a common heritage and a common historical function. For the Italians of the fifteenth century, every city had in itself something of that supreme, absolute ideological-historical-political reality which was the empire—it was more than a city, it was a state *in nuce*. The greatest historical city, where the idea of the empire had been realized, was ancient Rome. Now it was nothing but a memory. However, if at least four Italian cities could claim the honor of being Rome's direct heirs, almost all cities (not only in Italy) could claim to be descended from Roman cities. The problem of the reconstruction, or rather the rebirth, of Rome only arose about the middle of the fifteenth century; however, it was clear that from the beginning of the formation of humanistic culture the ideal model had been the political city, Rome as *urbs*, and no longer as *civitas*, or even less as *municipium*.

The first attempt at city planning conceived within the framework of a political program was due to the extreme importance of the historical factor. After Pisa's victory of 1063 at Palermo, which took supremacy over the Tyrrhenian Sea from the Saracen, she decided to increase in size. The new city center was planned outside the old walls, and work was begun on the chosen site in the form of the Cathedral, Baptistery, and Camposanto. Pisa could claim to have been founded in the Augustan period, and she jealously guarded her Roman juridical tradition. Later, in the thirteenth century, she became the chief center of an artistic culture (sculptor Nicola Pisano and architect Arnolfo di Cambio) which derived its inspiration directly from ancient Rome. The core of the new city (which was never built) would have followed the pattern of ancient Rome, with a complex of monuments to indicate the great ideological values which the city represented. Naturally those values had changed. For Christian Pisa, victorious over the Muslims in the name of the Faith, they were birth (the baptistery), life (the church), and death (the cemetery); however, these values had to be made clear by the solemn forms of the monumental complex (*Fig. 29*).

The Roman precedent is important for the clarification of an essential aspect of Renaissance city planning and the transformation of cities. The shape of a city depended on its monuments, taken as generations of urbanistic form, rather than on theories of the ideal city or on rational planning schemas. The idea of the monument was typically humanistic; the monument was a building which expressed and symbolized historical and ideological values of great moral importance for the community. It is thus that a single building can assume the importance of a symbol. The foremost monument of ancient Rome was the Coliseum, and it was, in fact, used as the typical *signum urbis* in medieval portrayals of the city (*Figs. 30–31*). Because of its size, its location, and the solemnity of its form, the monument assumed a dominant role in the context of the city; it became the focal point of Rome's urban perspective.

Filippo Brunelleschi (1377?–1446), at the beginning of the fifteenth century, was the first to deal with an architectonic problem—one of construction technique—in terms of city planning. The problem concerned the building of the dome over the Cathedral of Santa Maria del Fiore in Florence, which had been planned by Arnolfo di Cambio in the concluding years of the thirteenth century, and which had risen to the height of the drum during the next century (*Fig. 32*). Brunelleschi did not limit himself to dealing with the problem which seemed insurmountable to his contemporaries—that of vaulting a space of such huge diameter that traditional techniques were rendered useless. The need to construct such a vast dome had already been created in the first part of the fourteenth century when Giotto built a campanile beside the unfinished cathedral (*Fig. 33*). Giotto (1276?–1337?), who had acquired great prestige in fourteenth-century Florence, had wanted not only to give the cathedral its indispensable accessory but wished to build the campanile as an independent, symbolic structure. This can be seen clearly in the sculptured reliefs that adorn its walls, most of them designed by Giotto. The campanile was to be the symbol or insignia of a city renowned for the technical perfection of its artists and craftsmen. For this reason it rose up huge and isolated, like a beacon visible from every part of the city and marking its center. It was the ideal axis of Florence.

The symbolic and urbanistic importance of Giotto's bell tower was not lost on Brunelleschi, but, with the sense of history which is implicit in humanistic culture, he also realized that the current values of his city were no longer those that Giotto has exalted with the campanile. Florence was no longer merely a community of artisans and merchants; it was a financial power, a historical-political entity. Its culture was not characterized by an excellence in the *artes mechanicae*, but by the intellectual dignity of the *artes liberales*. A tall, linear construction like Giotto's tower could mark the center of a working community, enclosed within the ring of its ancient walls, but it could not represent the new historical reality of a city with cultural and political prestige, dominating vast territories. Hence it was necessary to construct a new form in order to express the new reality, and to give it a scale that would surpass the now outdated symbolism of the campanile. Alberti, another humanist who was extremely sensitive to the historical-symbolic meaning of architecture, pointed out the new ideological value expressed by the dome and praised it for its vastness, which enabled it to cover "with its shadow" not only the Florentine people but also "all the Tuscan peoples."

The dome was important for the new relationship it established with the volume of preexisting buildings, for the relationship between its form and its surroundings, and for the technique devised by Brunelleschi in order to close it without wooden falsework. Without doubt, the dome clearly terminated and unified the mass of the building; it equalized the contrasting forms of the nave and the apse, and it solved the whole play of forces in the extension of its curve in the capping form outlined against the free space of the sky (*Fig. 34*). Concluding at such a great height the edifice was not only related to surrounding civic buildings, but to the sky itself, which became so involved in the dimensions of city space. By bringing into equilibrium the Gothic dimensional disparities between various parts of the cathedral it immediately acquired a classical, monumental character.

Concerning the form, Brunelleschi himself declared that he wanted it to be as "full and magnificent" as possible, and he therefore proposed to give the great volume of the dome an effect of lightness which would free it, like a huge balloon, in the open sky above the city (*Fig. 38*). The formal and technical devices on which the architect relied to obtain this dual effect are well known; it is enough to say here that the very ribbing which gave tension and energy to the dome clearly formed a perspective structure, and that perspective was for Brunelleschi the universal structure of space. A perspective cupola was not merely an object situated in space; it was a form which represented all space and therefore had a theoretically infinite capacity (*Fig. 36*). For this reason the dome is the ideal cover for the whole city, relating Florence to the horizon of the surrounding hills on which the natural dome of the sky seems to rest (*Fig. 37*). Of course a form conceived as a solid or plastic pivot of the constant position of physical space could not be static, a spherical bowl pressing down heavily on the walls of the church. It had to be a form with an internal dynamism, capable of sustaining itself and tying into natural space in a rotative sense suggested by its ribs and by the planes that are formed radially around the latern (*Fig. 35*) like the spokes of a wheel.

From the point of view of the technical construction, the dome is a completely new thing which transformed not only traditional methods of work but the very social organization of the building trade as well. It is well known that before undertaking the technical problem of construction Brunelleschi went to Rome to study the fabric and proportions of the ancient city walls. However, it is clear that, although the dome of Santa Maria del Fiore implied a familiarity with ancient methods, it was not built in a traditional manner. It is thus a modern invention based on historical research. Evidently Brunelleschi thought that a new technique could not be derived from the past, but must come from a different cultural experience, from history. In this way he refuted the old "mechanical" technique and created a new "liberal" technique based on those typically individualistic actions which are historical research and inventiveness. He abolished the traditional hierarchical form of the mason's lodge where the head was the coordinator of the specialized work of the various groups of skilled workers who made up the lodge masters. Now there was only one planner or inventor; the others were merely manual laborers. When the master mason rose to the status of sole planner, whose activity was on a par with the other humanistic disciplines, the other members of the team of masons fell from the rank of *maestri* in charge of various aspects of the job to that of simple working men. This explains the impatience of the masons and their rebellion against the master mason who had become an "architect" or "engineer."

The consequence of this—its importance also in the field of city planning—could be seen already in other works by Brunelleschi. He used the classical architectural morphology of equal, repetitive elements almost in series and eliminated the abundant Gothic decoration that had generally been carried out in the masons' workshop (*Figs. 39–40*). Architectural elements such as columns, capitals, cornices, and so on, could now be constructed outside the shop and then put in place according to the architect's design, just as prefabricated elements are used today. This saved an enormous amount of time, both in the planning and in the execution. It was now possible to plan major works with a good probability of seeing them completed within a few years. Even with delays caused by unforeseen circumstances, the construction could be carried out according to the plan of the original architect; a great construction need no longer be the work of successive generations, but of a single artist. If it became possible in the Renaissance to think of the city as a unified form (in a utopian but not absurd manner), willed into being by a prince and created by his architect, this was due to the changes in the methods of planning and execution begun by Brunelleschi, which made it theoretically possible to construct a city within a man's lifetime.

Leon Battista Alberti (1404–1472) had already expressed the idea of a building as being representative of great cultural values and serving as an urban generator—the typically humanistic concept of "monument." Naturally a cathedral or a municipal palace of the fourteenth century embodied the ideal values of the whole community (*Fig. 41*); but, in the context of the new humanistic culture, ideal values were essentially of a historical nature and referred back to a great past—more precisely to ancient Rome—to which most Italian cities owed their beginnings.

Alberti lived in Rome for a long while, as Latin secretary (*abbreviatore apostolico*) at the papal curia. Before his eyes lay the desolate sight of a great, lost civilization and of a city, once famous for its glory, reduced to ruins. Nor had a new city arisen above the remains of the old. At the beginning of the fifteenth

26

century Rome was still a mass of wretched houses huddled in a bend in the river Tiber. Even the great basilicas of early Christendom were in ruins; recent religious and political disturbances—the Schism, the absence of the seat of the Papacy, the quarrels between factions in the city—had aggravated the condition of neglect and poverty. It was only toward the middle of the fifteenth century, when a humanist pope, Nicholas V (pontificate, 1447–1455), succeeded in putting an end to the Schism, reaffirming the historical priority and preeminent authority of the Church of Rome, and bringing the apostolic seat back to the city, that the need to give Rome an appearance worthy of her past became urgent. The thought of the great ancient city in ruins was an essential factor leading to the formation of the concept of a *forma urbis* in the Italian Renaissance. This was particularly true in Alberti's case, since he lived at the court of the humanist pope. Alberti was not a builder, but he believed that the duty of a humanist was not to commemorate a lost civilization but to join in the recreating of it. He became a restorer of ancient monuments, an architect and a theoretician. His basic treatise, *De re aedificatoria* (1443–1452), was essentially an attempt to reconstruct a theoretical foundation for the long-desired *restauratio urbis Romae* by referring back to Vitruvius.

It has been amply shown that the personality of Alberti as an architect was far more complex and original than evidenced in his theoretical writings. It was not lack of technical knowledge that made Alberti examine more closely and theorize about the distinction already made by Brunelleschi between planning and execution of plans, emphasizing that the planner must not concern himself with the material realization of his projects. The architect was above all a man of culture and, as such, he had a direct, exclusive relationship with political and religious authority. His duty was to *conceive* the form of the buildings, a form which carried ideas. It was his responsibility, then, to summon up the "monuments" which made up the heart of the city, and on which both the historical and ideological symbolism rested. The Tempio Malatestiano in Rimini (*Fig. 45*), the churches of Sant'Andrea (*Fig. 46*) and San Sebastiano in Mantua, the Palazzo Rucellai (*Fig. 47*) and the rotunda of the Annunziata in Florence were all so conceived, and were consequently of vital importance to the fabric of the city. The historical-ideological values of a monument were the precise ones on which the historical-social function of the city was based. The facade which Alberti projected for the Dominican church of Santa Maria Novella in Florence (originally built at the end of the thirteenth century) is evidence that he considered this monument of the past to be valid within the framework of the new culture and appropriate for inclusion in the historical reality of Florence in his own day (*Fig. 44*).

In Italian society of the fifteenth century, authority was concentrated in the *signore*, but relied on the relatively broad base of great families, religious orders, and cultural bodies. What made a city "historical" was its extraordinary accumulation of cultural assets such as universities, libraries, collections of antiquities, works of art, and the like which were both a valuable heritage and a source of political authority. Monumental value belonged, then, not only to the cathedral and town hall, but to all those edifices which together produced the city's tone of urbanity. Alberti declared that the palaces of nobles need not resemble fortresses to be impressive, but should be distinguished by their harmonious proportions and the fineness of their ornamentation: They were to express the social prestige of the family, but as based on cultural values and not on force. In fifteenth-century Florence there arose numerous patrician palaces which represented the contribution of the ruling class to the historical character of the modern city. But these palaces were not the only decisive influence on Florentine and Tuscan city form. If Brunelleschi was asked to give an artistic form to an orphanage (*Ospedale degli Innocenti*), it was because the social and charitable functions of a hospital for abandoned infants were considered part of the system of urban culture. Brunelleschi developed the theme of *orphanage* "urbanistically," making legible from the outside the internal spatial qualities of the edifice and including in the facade the opening of two streets thereby making the frontal plane of the building a plane of perspective intersection with the space of the piazza (*Fig. 40*).

Of course, if the function of the "monument" is to manifest certain ideal values by means of architectural form, it is necessary to guarantee the best conditions for viewing such buildings from near or far. Of fundamental importance, then, are the position of the building in the urban fabric and the conditions of perspective or viewpoint. A building which is given monumental character influences a rather vast portion of the city. It tended, for example, not only to modify the layout of streets, so that it could be most accessible and visible, but also to raise the architectural tone of the whole surrounding quarter. And since a structure of monumental character tended also to be bigger than the others, it resulted in a new and larger scale, adapting the dimensions of the open spaces, streets and squares to its own volume. So it is that perspective, as a theoretical construction of space, became also the primary regulator of the urban network in the Italian Renaissance.

# SPECIFIC EXAMPLES

## PIENZA, FERRARA, VIGEVANO

Two great urbanistic enterprises were designed and partially realized during the second half of the fifteenth century: the transformation of the farming village of Corsignano into a city (Pienza) by the Florentine architect Bernardo Rossellino (1409–1464) at the initiative of Pope Pius II Piccolomini (pontificate, 1458–1464), and the enlargement or "doubling" of Ferrara with the *addizione erculea* at the behest of Prince Ercole I d'Este as carried out by Biagio Rossetti.

The transformation of a country village into a city of noblest architectural character was not brought about by economic, social, or political necessity; it was the intellectual whim of a humanist pope, convinced that in this way he could make his birthplace famous. The new city of Pienza consisted simply of a few patrician palaces arranged in a perspective relationship to the cathedral (*Figs. 22–24*). For the most part they were palaces which cardinals of the papal curia were compelled to build against their will to keep in favor with the Pope. The cathedral itself was not conceived as the sacred center of the community, but as a metaphysical space constructed (following in this case Alberti's thesis) according to mathematical rules of proportion. The two lateral walls of the cathedral square were formed by the Bishop's palace (Palazzo Vescovile) and the Palazzo Piccolomini, whose facades were not parallel but diverged as they approached the front of the cathedral (*Fig. 24*). The perspective construction was in this way adjusted optically in order to emphasize the breadth of the cathedral facade. This solution (similar to the one used by Michelangelo in the Piazza del Campidoglio in Rome) is important because it showed that the interest of the architect was no longer concentrated on single buildings, but on the open space of the square as outlined by their facades (cf. *Figs. 23, 59*). The architectural form, therefore, was not that of a solid volume whose facades suggested the internal structure, but a cubic void whose facades are the enclosing walls. The space of the city was conceived, then, as an "interior," and, more precisely, as the interior of a palace in which the squares were the rooms and the streets were corridors and staircases. Rossellino was an architect for whom city planning was no more than an extension of architecture and

the city was a building formed from the perspective and proportional combination of several buildings.

A typical urbanist—in fact, the first city planner in the modern
sense—was Biagio Rossetti. The decision made by Prince
Ercole I d'Este in 1492 to double the area of Ferrara (*Fig. 48*)
was based on a number of practical considerations: strategic, to
improve defense to the north (where the power of neighboring
Venice was a constant threat); demographic, to increase the
power of the duchy without increasing the already overcrowded population in the old city; economic, to increase the
economy of the exchange carried out by immigrant Jews. The
suture between the old city and the Extension (*addizione erculea*) was obtained by filling in the Giovecca moat, which fixed
the boundaries of the built-up area to the north, and then by
transforming it into the main axial street of the enlarged city
(*Figs. 49, 51*). The reconstruction and analysis that Zevi has
made of Rossetti's plan (see Appendix: Ferrara) has shown
that: 1) Rossetti, while putting the prince's plan into operation,
began from an accurate analysis of the actual city and of its
possibilities for coherent development; 2) the study culminated
in the design of an extremely elastic city system, which allowed
for the final definition, point by point, of the building solutions;
3) the plan had been elaborated on concrete evidence free of
any a priori theory and with constant concern not to err in the
direction of either "abstract rationalization" or "banal empiri-
cism"; 4) the aim was to link the streets of the Extension one by
one to the communication channels of the medieval city,
establishing a social continuity between the old and the new
sectors; 5) the plan was not intended to turn the new defensive
ring of walls into a barrier that would constrict further development of the city, but to substitute the so-called "bastionated
front," arranged according to the accidents of topography, for
the rigid geometric type of fortifications.

Only after deciding on the dimensions of his city did Rossetti
go on to study the architectural attributes one by one; in this
way he succeeded in reconciling the regularity of the layout
with the character of the different building sites (*Figs. 50,52*). It
was an attitude diametrically opposed to that of Rossellino who,
in Pienza, started with an architectural unity in order to arrive,
by extension, at the urban whole. Another important factor was
the autonomy of Rossetti's city plan with respect to Ercole's
political plan. In fact, as Zevi has observed, Rossetti's plan for

Ferrara retained its full validity, controlling the development of the city up to the present, although Ercole's political plan, which made Rossetti's work possible, was never carried out.

A sharply antithetical solution, indicative of the authoritarian nature of the *signori*, was conceived by Lodovico il Moro for Vigevano and carried out with the help of Bramante (as has been demonstrated). By demolishing part of the old city center, a huge porticoed square was created which became both the largest square of the city and a kind of external courtyard to the ducal palace. It was, *in nuce*, the solution adopted for royal palaces in the seventeenth century, during the period of absolute monarchism.

## ROME

The problem of replanning the city of Rome, already considered by Alberti in the middle of the fifteenth century, was only dealt with in concrete terms in the century that followed (*Figs. 53–54*). The history of Rome's *cinquecento* reorganization was of fundamental importance for the influence it would exert on the configuration of the great capitals of Europe. The city which already symbolized religious authority was to become the model of the city representing political power (*Figs. 67–70*).

The thesis of Rome's reclamation through the recovery, the restoration, and the insertion of ancient monuments into the city fabric was clearly reaffirmed in a "report to Leo X," attributed by some to Raphael and by others to Bramante. In essence it held that ancient Rome still existed as *"la macchina del tutto, ma senza ornamenti, et per dir cosi, l'ossa del corpe senze carne"* (the mechanism underlying all things, but unadorned, almost one might say, like the bones of the body without flesh). Hence the need to rebuild at least those monuments in which the parts that were still standing allowed one to reconstruct the missing elements. The proposal led to nothing more than intense activity in published drawings of ancient monuments, but this did lead to the formation of a repertory, almost a vocabulary of ancient architectural forms, which were put to great use especially in the latter half of the sixteenth century. The reconstruction of Rome, begun under the patronage of Julius II (pontificate, 1503–1513), and continued later by Leo X (pontificate, 1513–1521), was rudely interrupted by the increased intensity of the religious and political struggle which in 1527 led to the siege and sack of the city. When work began again in the second half of the

1. Bologna, airview of the city center showing the Asinelli and Carisenda towers (at center). In the thirteenth and fourteenth centuries, the urban landscape of Italy was characterized by many tall elements, tower houses built by leading families, who as leaders of various parties were constantly struggling against one another.
2. Perugia, a street in the medieval city.

3. Siena, *Good Government*, a fresco by Ambrogio Lorenzetti, Palazzo Pubblico, 1337–1339. The relationship between the city and the surrounding countryside is portrayed with great clarity.
4. A section of the "City of Vitruvius," in the reconstruction by Cesare Cesariano, 1452.

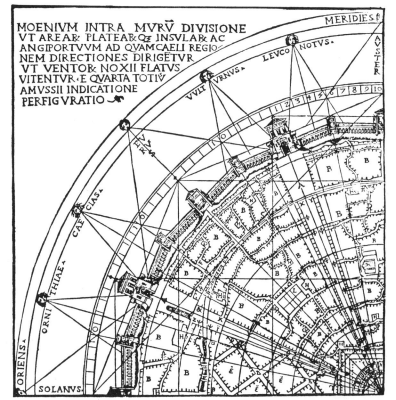

MOENIVM INTRA MVRV DIVISIONE
VT AREAⱹ PLATEAⱹQⱬ INSVLAⱹ AC
ANGIPORTVVM AD QVAMCAELI REGIO
NEM DIRECTIONES DIRIGETVR
VT VENTOⱹ NOXII FLATVS
VITENTVR·E QVARTA TOTIV̄
AMVSSII INDICATIONE
PERFIGVRATIO

5. Plan of an ideal city, Sforzinda, by Filarete, 1464.
6. Plan of city on a plain, by Francesco di Giorgio Martini, 1451–1464.
7. Plan of a city on a hill, by Francesco di Giorgio Martini, 1451–1464.

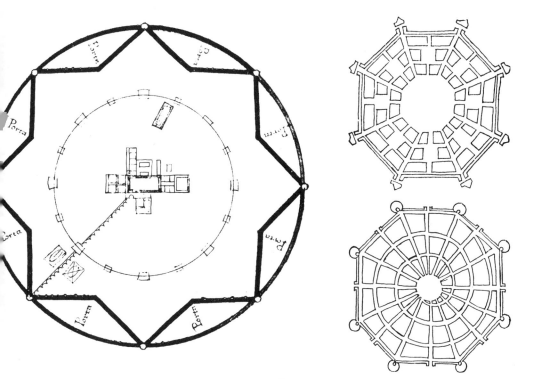

8. Plan of a fortified ideal city, crossed by a river, from the *Codice Magliabecchiano*, by Francesco di Giorgio Martini, 1451–1464.
9. Plan of an ideal city, by Francesco di Giorgio Martini, 1451–1464.

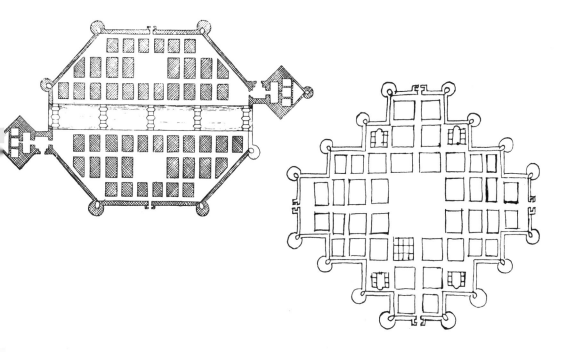

10. Plan of an ideal city, by Albrecht Dürer, 1527.
11. Freudenstadt, plan by Heinrich Schickhardt, 1632.
12. Plan of an ideal city from the *Architecture of Fortifications*, by Daniel Speckle, 1589.

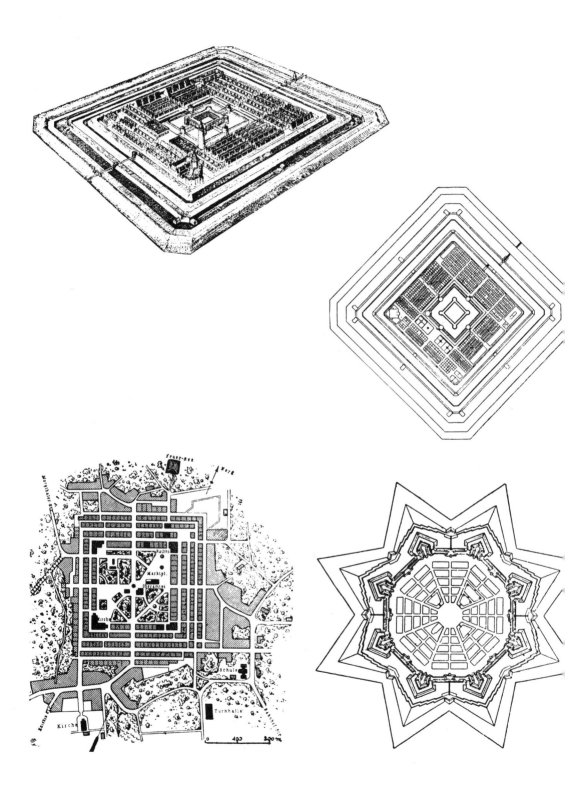

13. San Leo (near Pesaro). The fortress ascribed to Francesco di Giorgio Martini, after 1482.
14. San Leo, the fortress.

15. Volterra, the Rocca Nuova, 1472. With its round bastions, it is still basically medieval.
16. Civita Castellana, the fortress, by Antonio da Sangallo the Elder, with the octagonal "keep," by Antonio da Sangallo the Younger. The younger Sangallo was one of the sixteenth-century innovators of military architecture.

17. Florence, study for the fortifications of the city, by Michelangelo, 1529.
18. Florence, study for the fortifications of the city, by Michelangelo, 1529.

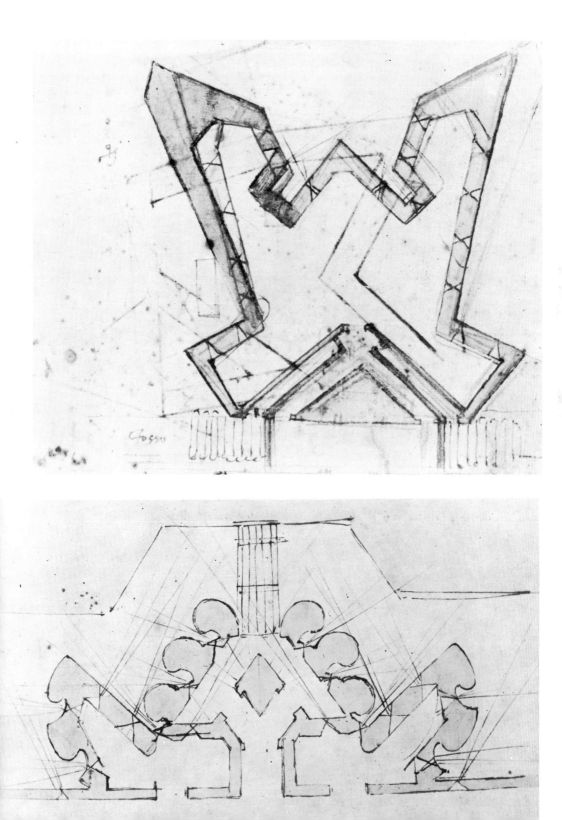

19. Urbino, view of the Palazzo Ducale, fifteenth
    century.
20. Urbino, Palazzo Ducale, the "Torricini"
    facade, designed c. 1465.

21. Naples, Arch of Alfonso of Aragon adorning the Castel Nuovo, 1453–1467.
22. Pienza, the square and the cathedral, c. 1460.

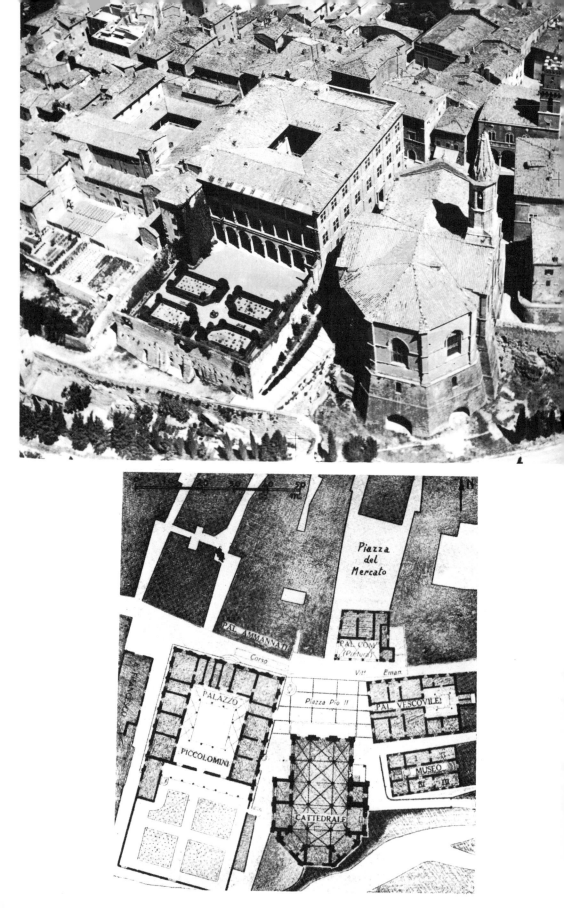

PIAZZA del Mercato

PAL. AMMANNATI

PAL. COM (Pretura)

Corso

Vitt. Eman.

FRANCESCO

PALAZZO

PICCOLOMINI

Piazza Pio II

PAL. VESCOVILE

MUSEO

CATTEDRALE

Pienza, airview of the town center.
Pienza, schematic plan of the monumental center of the city.

25. View of a square in an ideal city, painting, late fifteenth century.
26. View of an ideal city beside the sea, painting, fifteenth century.

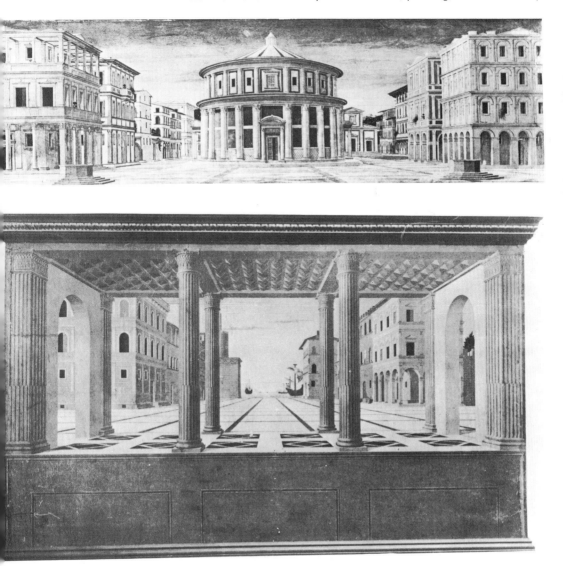

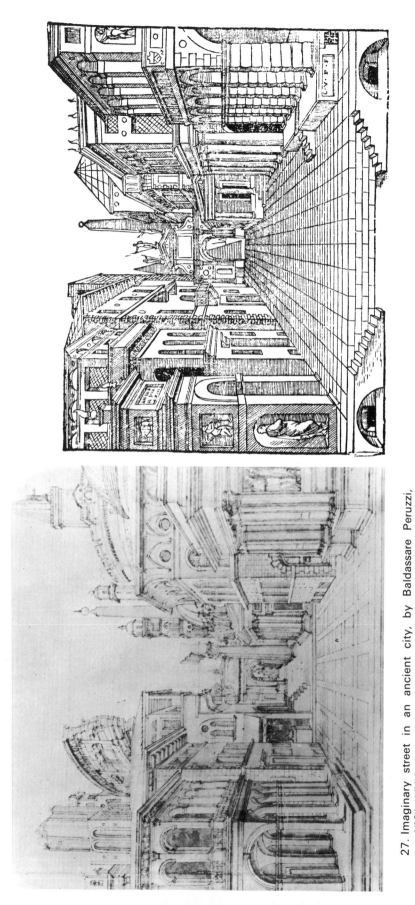

27. Imaginary street in an ancient city, by Baldassare Peruzzi, 1481–1536. The drawing is of scenery for the tragic theater.

28. A street "in ancient style" for a tragic scene, from *I sette libri di architettura*, by Sebastiano Serlio, 1537–1557.

29. Pisa, airview of the Campo dei Miracoli with the cathedral, leaning tower, baptistery, and cemetery.

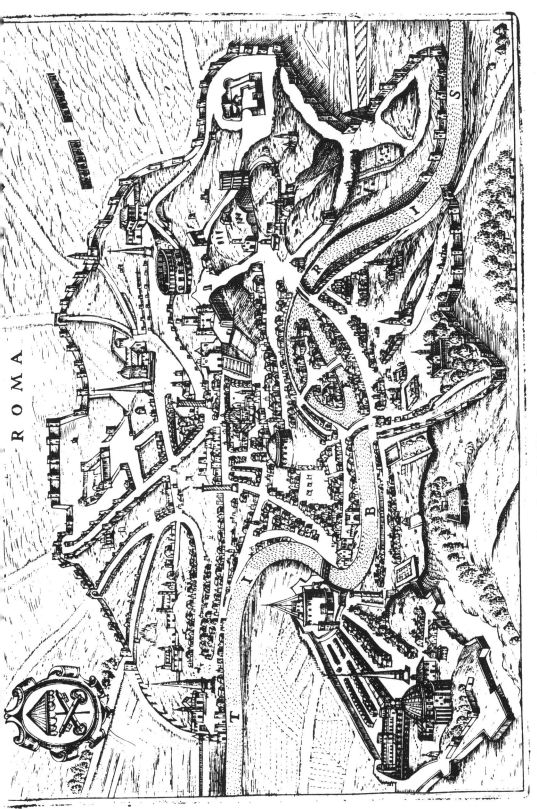

31. Rome, a sixteenth-century view by Pietro Bertelli, 1599.

32. Florence, the cathedral appearing as an allegorical symbol of the

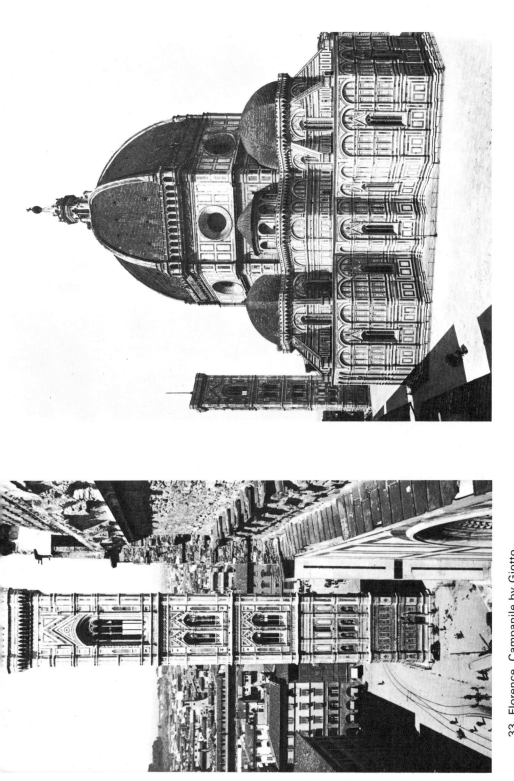

33. Florence, Campanile by Giotto.
34. Florence, the Cathedral of Santa Maria del Fiore. Note the relationship between the apses and the dome.

35. Florence, the lantern of the cathedral. With the halo shape of the lantern, marking the axis of the dome, Brunelleschi had wanted to emphasize the dome as the pivot of city space.

36. Florence, airview of the city center showing the cathedral, bell tower, and baptistery.
37. Florence, the cathedral in relation to the urban landscape.

38. Florence at the end of the fifteenth century, print.

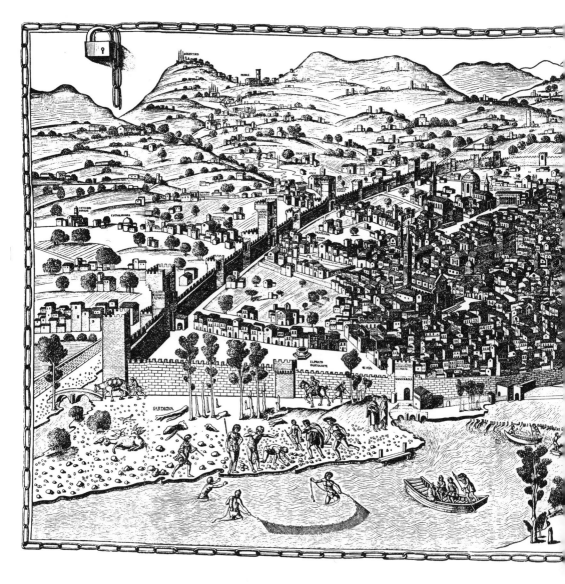

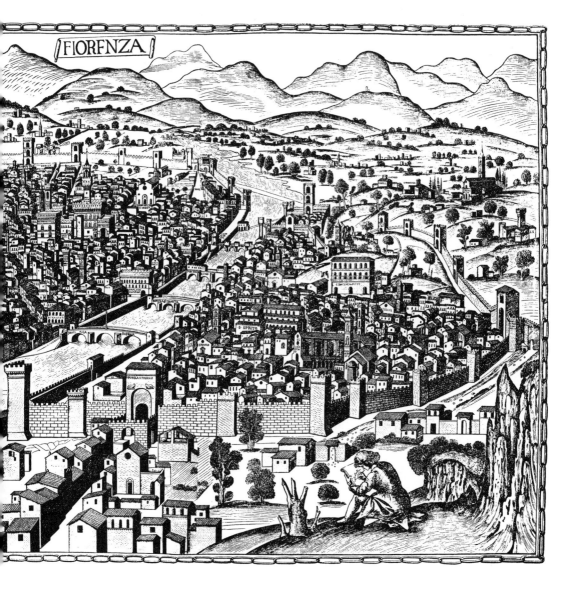

39. Florence, Bosignori plan, 1584.

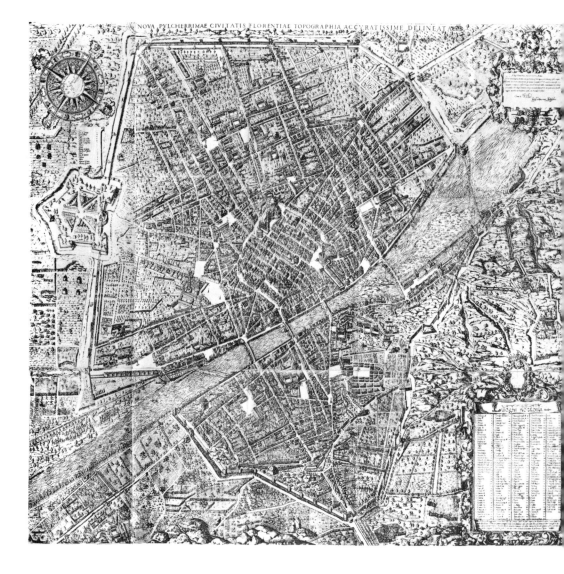

40. Florence, the square of SS. Annunziata, with the Ospedale degli Innocenti, designed by Brunelleschi in 1419.
41. Florence, Palazzo Pitti, designed c. 1440.

42. Florence, the street which joins the Piazza della Signoria to the Lungarno (between the two wings of the Uffizi), by Giorgio Vasari, 1565.
43. Florence, Ponte Santa Trinità, by Bartolomeo Ammanati, 1567–1570.

44. Florence, Santa Maria Novella, the facade, by Leon Battista Alberti, 1470.
45. Rimini, Tempio Malatestiano, by Leon Battista Alberti, begun c. 1446.

46. Mantua, Sant'Andrea, designed by Leon Battista Alberti, 1470.
47. Florence, Palazzo Rucellai, by Leon Battista Alberti, 1446–1451.

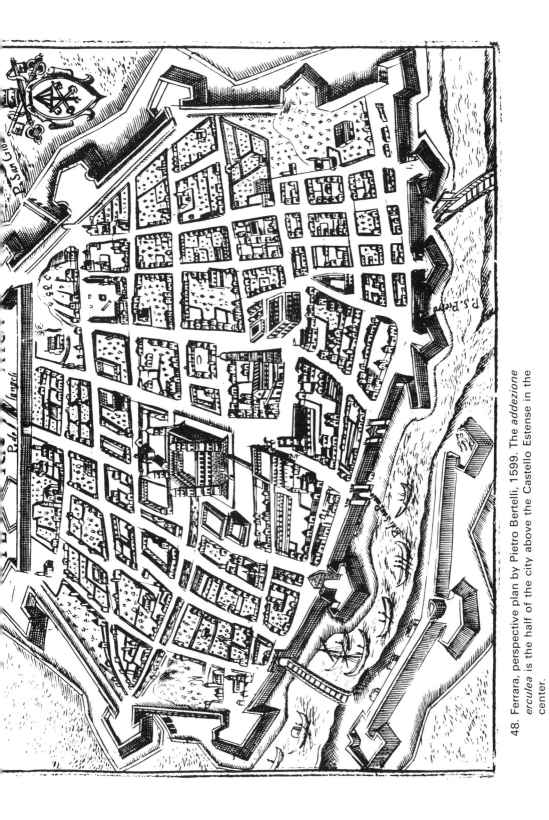

48. Ferrara, perspective plan by Pietro Bertelli, 1599. The *addezione erculea* is the half of the city above the Castello Estense in the center.

49. Ferrara, plan by Aleotti, 1605. The new Extension is above the
    Strada detta la Giovecca.
50. Ferrara, airview. The Extension is the upper half of the illustration
    above the straight line of the filled-in Giovecca Moat.

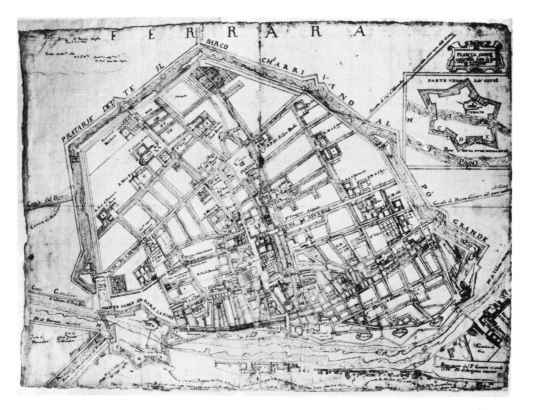

51. Ferrara, Piazza Nuova of the *addizione erculean*, c. 1500. This can be seen in the upper center of Figs. 48–49.
52. Ferrara, Palazzo Diamanti in *addizione erculean*, by Biagio Rosetti, 1492–1575.

53. Rome, airview. The Pantheon is at the center, the Ponte Sisto is the third from the bottom, the Via Giulia can be seen running north from the Ponte Sisto and the hospital of Santo Spirito is in the upper-left corner.
54. Rome, airview. The "trident" of the Piazza del Popolo.

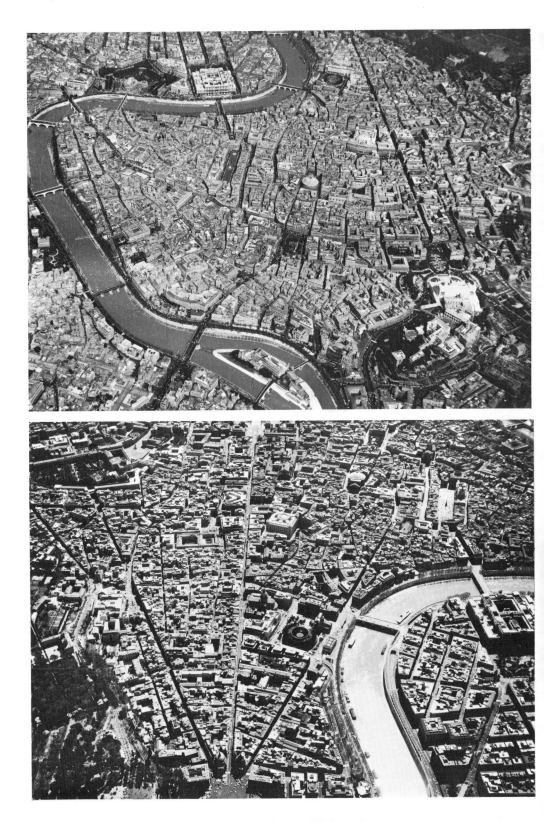

55. Two types of nobles' residences, at the beginning of the sixteenth century, Rome. (a) residence built by Bramante for Raphael, in a print by Lafreri; (b) the Palazzo Branconio dell'Aquila, designed by Raphael.
56. Rome, view from St. Peter's, by Gaspare van Wittel, 1653–1736.

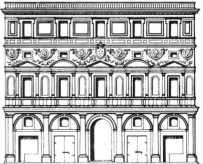

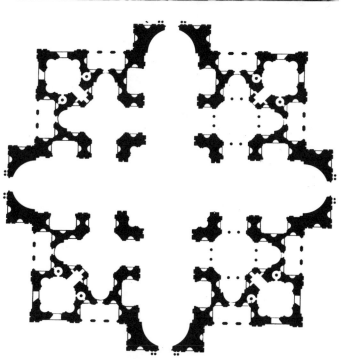

58. Rome, plan for St. Peter's, by Bramante, 1506.
59. Rome, airview of St. Peter's.

60. Rome, plan of the Piazza del Campidoglio.
61. Rome, airview of the Piazza del Campidoglio, showing the ramp
   leading up to the piazza.

62. Rome, airview of the Piazza del Campidoglio.
63. Rome, airview of the Piazza del Campidoglio. Note the statue of Marcus Aurelius.

64. Rome, airview of the Via Pia (now Via XX Settembre) which runs vertically alongside the gardens to the right. The Porta Pia is out of view at the top.
65. Rome, schematic view of the roads laid out in the plan of Sixtus V, in a print by G. F. Bordino.

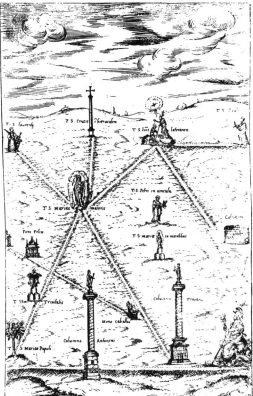

66. Rome, airview of Santa Maria Maggiore and the radiating streets of the plan of Sixtus V (cf. Fig. 65).
67. Rome, imaginary view according to the plan of Sixtus V, fresco, Biblioteca Apostolica, Vaticana.

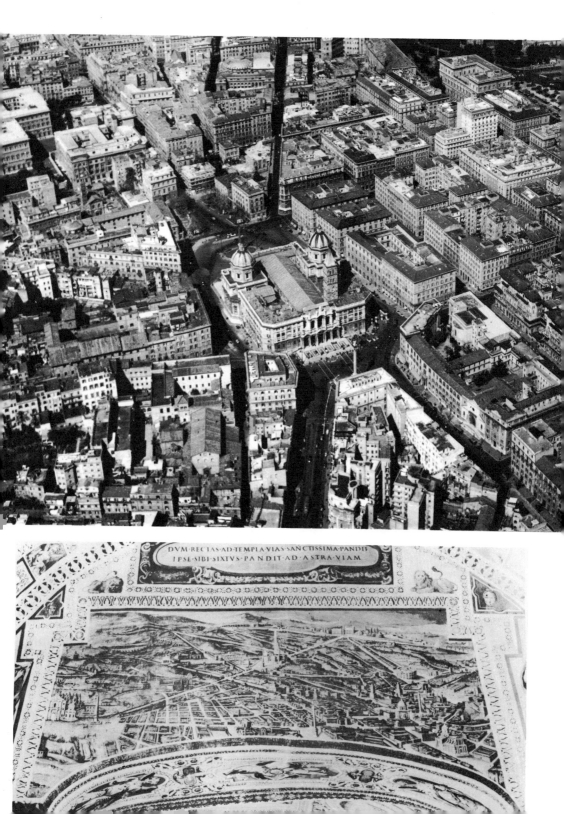

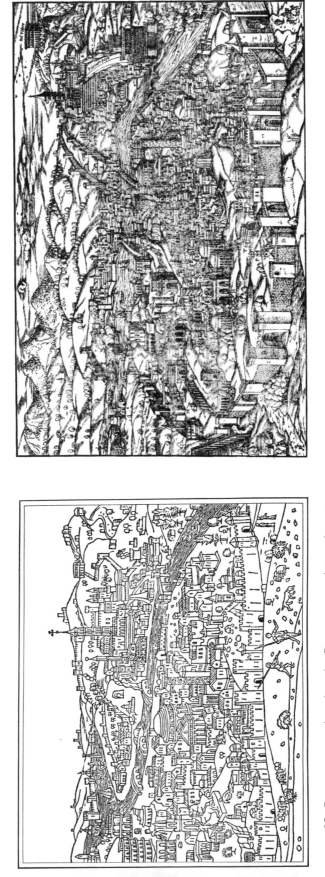

68. Rome, perspective view, by Bergomense, sixteenth century.
69. Rome, perspective view, by Munster, 1549.

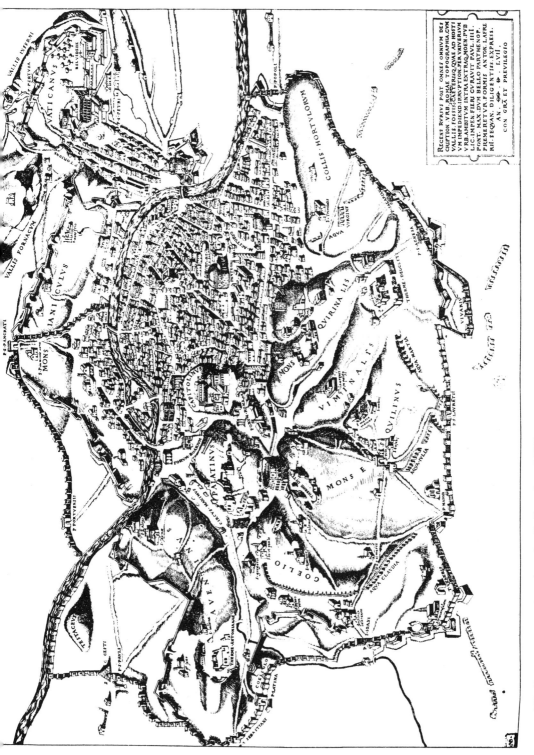

70. Rome, perspective view, by N. Beatrizet, 1557.

71. Rome, perspective view, by F. Paciotto, 1557.
72. Venice, perspective view, from Bertelli, 1599.

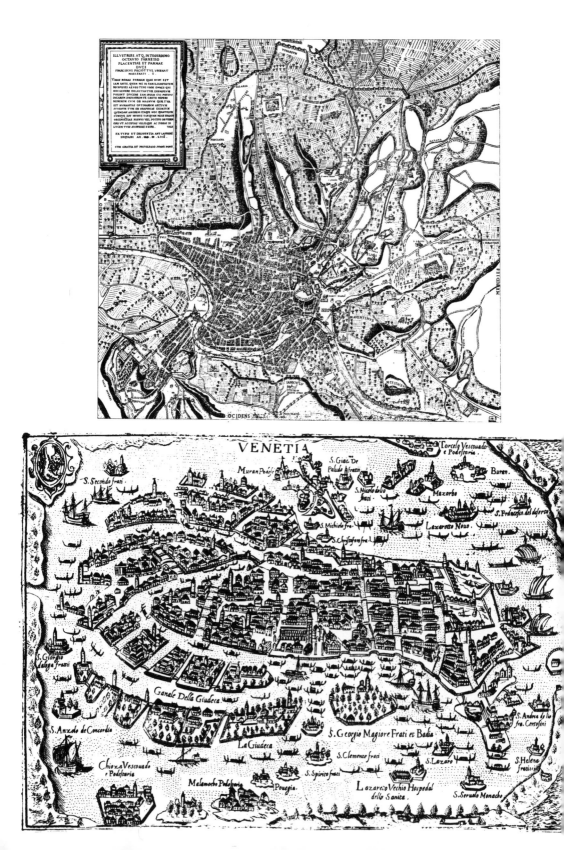

73. Venice, the basin of San Marco and the Island of San Giorgio, showing Andrea Palladio's church, San Giorgio Maggiore.
74. Venice, airview of Piazza San Marco.

75. Venice, plan for the Ponte di Rialto, from the trattato by Andrea Palladio, 1554.
76. Vicenza, a perspective street, designed as scenery for the Teatro Olimpico, by Andrea Palladio, 1580.

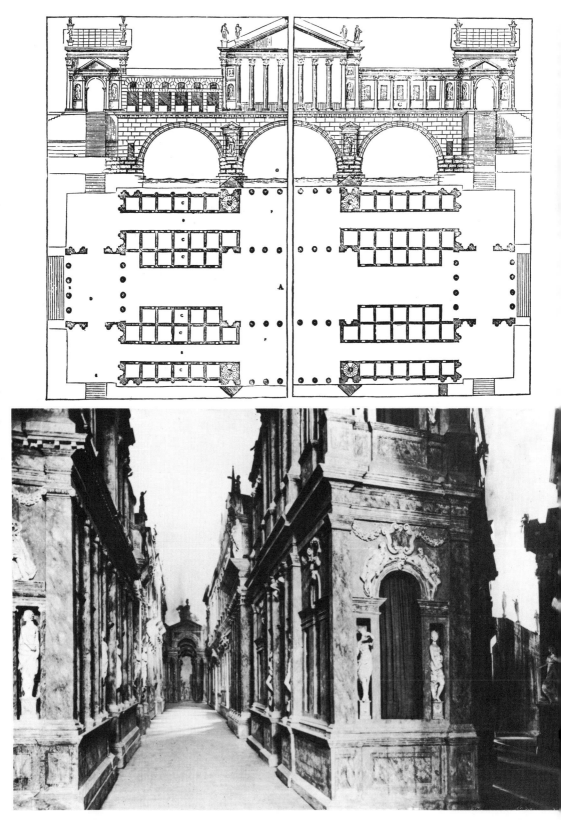

78. Sabbioneta, the Piazza Maggiore. Facing is the Ducal Palace of the late sixteenth century.
79. Sabbioneta, Piazza Maggiore seen from the Ducal Palace. On the left is the Church of S. Maria Assunta, constructed by Pietro Martire Pesenti, 1581.

80. Palmanova (in Fruili), a schematic plan, from Bertelli, 1599.
81. Palmanova, airview.

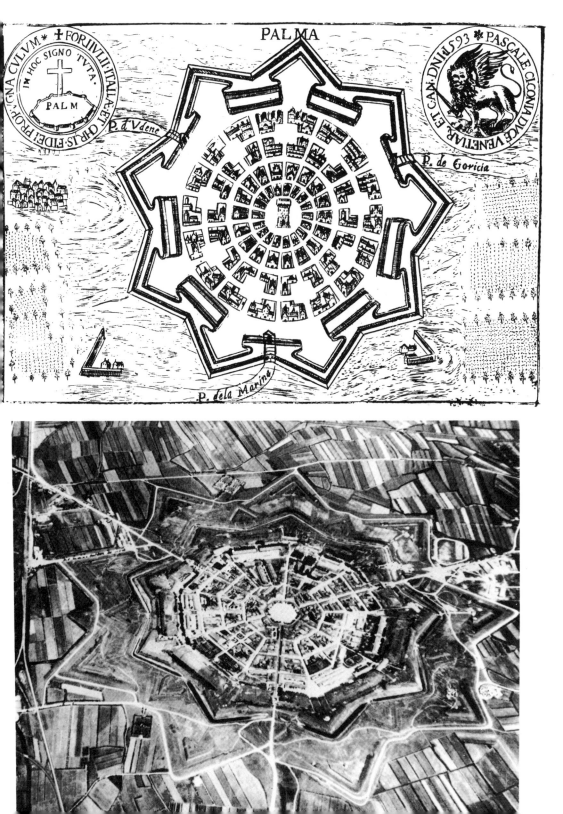

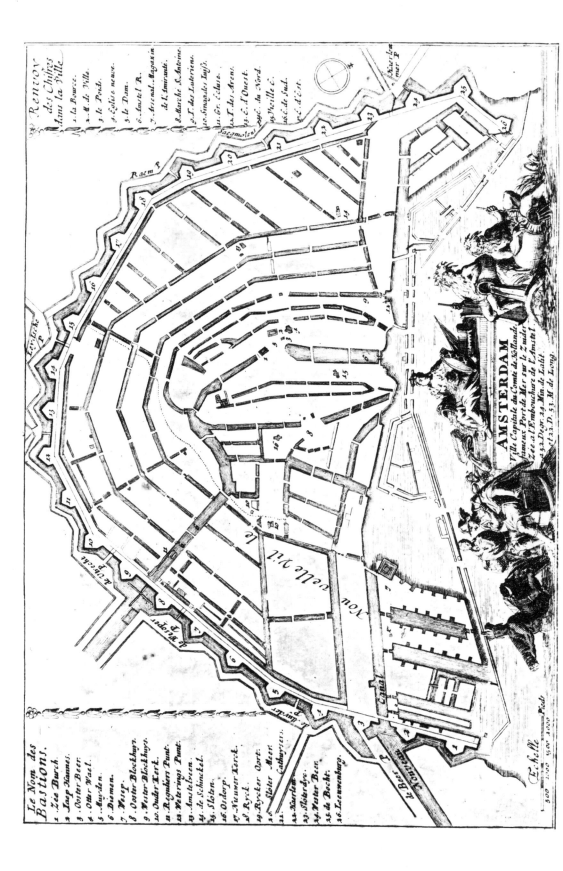

Le Nom des Bastions.

1. Zee Burch.
2. Jaep Hannes.
3. Ooster-Beer.
4. Otter-Waal.
5. Aarden.
6. Diemen.
7. Weesp.
8. Ooster-Blockhuys.
9. Wester-Blockhuys.
10. Ouder-Kerk.
11. Reguliers Punt.
12. Weterings Punt.
13. Amstelveen.
14. de Schinkel.
15. Sloten.
16. Osdorp.
17. Nieuwer-Kerck.
18. Ryck.
19. Rycker Oort.
20. Meter-Meer.
21. Catthuysers.
22. Haarlem.
23. Sloter-dye.
24. Vuter-Been.
25. de Becht.
26. Leeuwenburg.

Renvoy des Chifres dans la Ville.

1. la Bourse.
2. M. de Ville.
3. le Poids.
4. Eglise neuve.
5. le Dam.
6. Amstel R.
7. Arcenal. Magazin
   de l'Amirauté.
8. Marche S. Antoine.
9. E. des Luteriens.
10. Simandos Luyff.
11. Gr. Ecluse.
12. T. des Arens.
13. C. à l'Ouest.
14. Vec. du Nord.
15. Vieille c.
16. C. de Sud.
17. C. d'est.

Raem P.

Leydsche P.

à l'Ubezak P.

Wytert P.

de Buer P. de Nouveau

Canal

Nouvelle V. M.

Haarlem mer P.

AMSTERDAM

Ville Capitale du Comté de Hollande,
fameux Port de Mer sur le Zuider
Zee, à l'Embouchure de l'Amstel.
432. Deg. 24. Min. de Latit.
4 22. D. 53. M. de Long.

Echelle Pieds.
500 1000 1500 2000

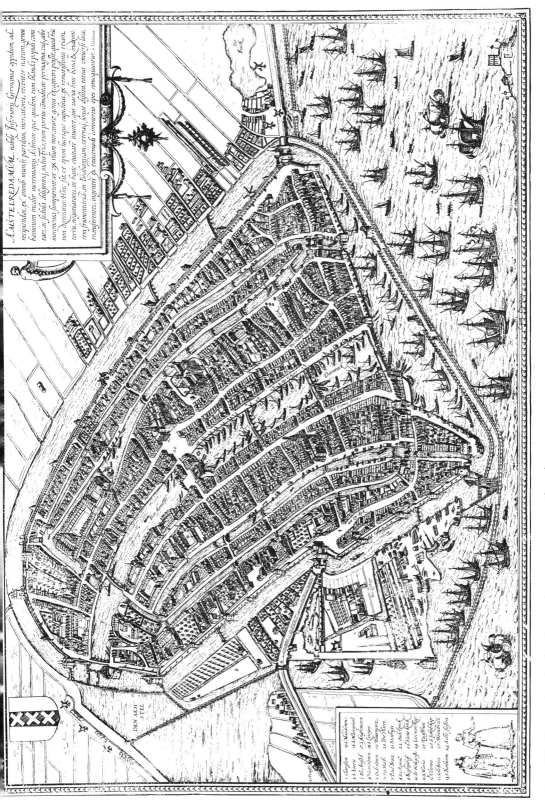

83. Amsterdam in the sixteenth century, perspective view.

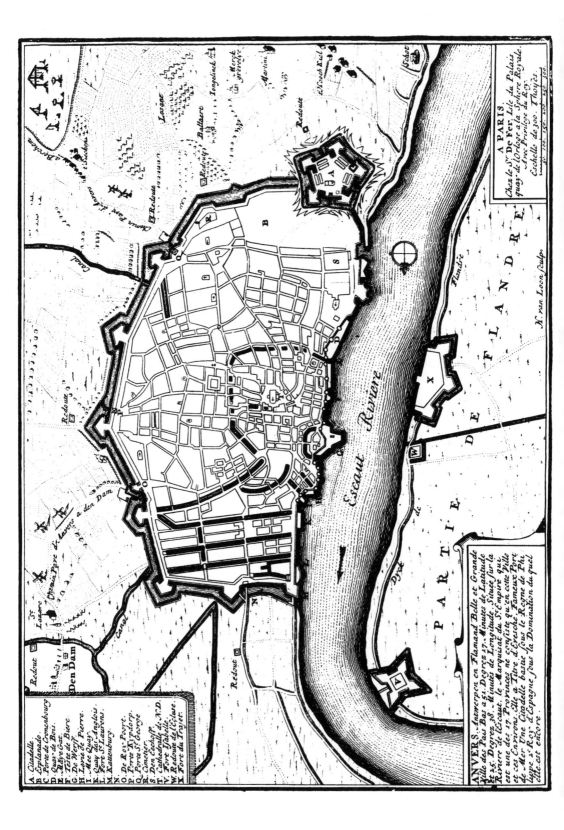

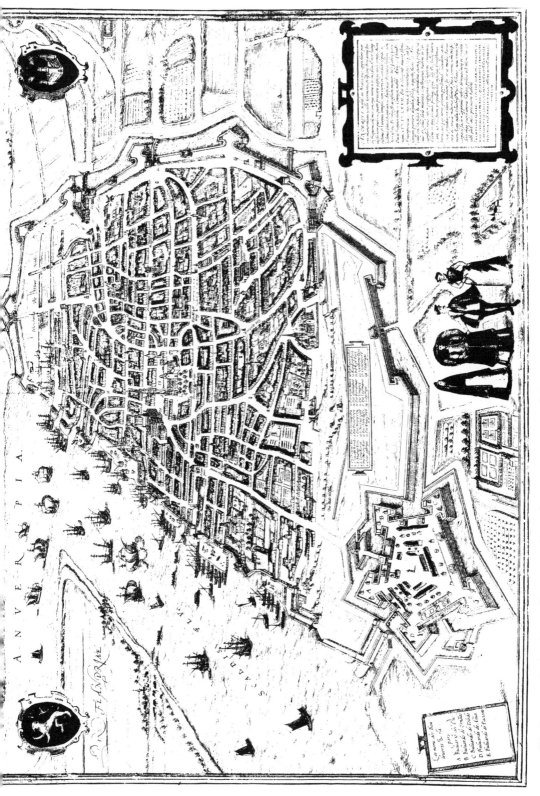

85. Antwerp, in the sixteenth century, shown in a contemporary print.

86. Cambridge, plan of the city, in 1688.
87. Cambridge, plan of Queen's College.

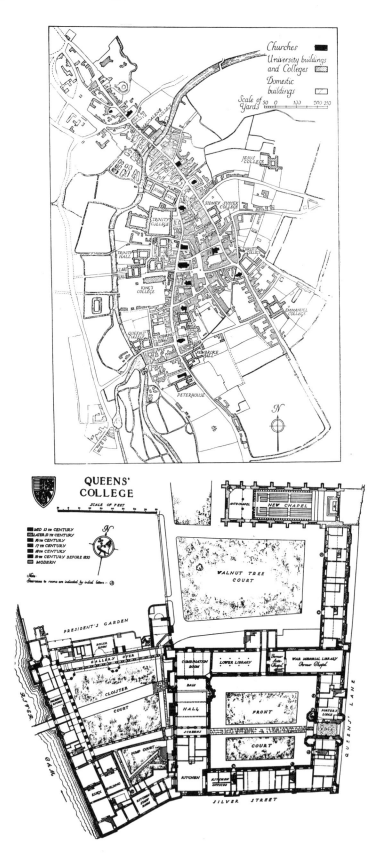

88. Civitavecchia, plan, from De Fer, 1645.
89. Geneva, plan, c. 1715.

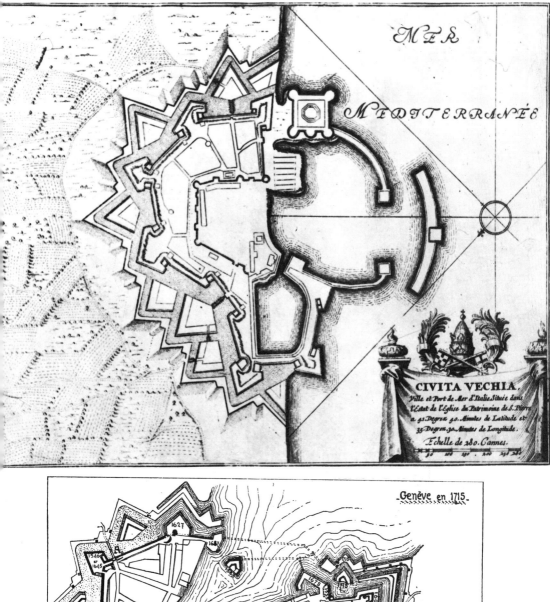

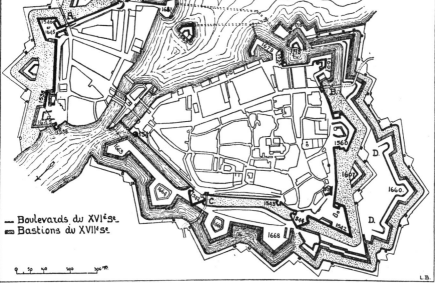

90. Genoa, Via Aurea (later Strada Nuova, now Via Garibaldi), shown
    in an eighteenth-century print.
91. Genoa, plan from Bertelli, 1599.

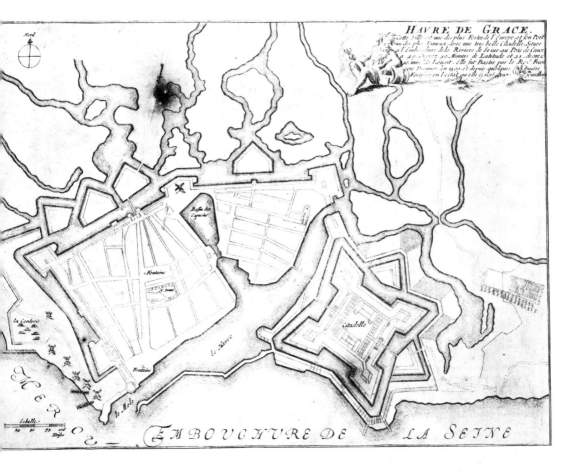

93. Hesdin, plan.
94. Leghorn, plan of the port and the fortifications, from De Fer,
    1645.

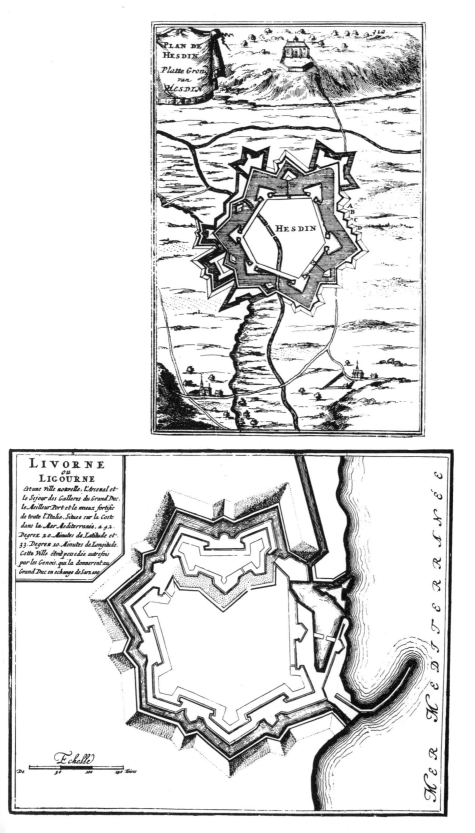

LAVRETVM

LAVRETVM. AGRIRECE-
NATENINITALIA CELEBRE
OPP:AD MARIÆ. ATIQVISSI
MAIEISITA Æ DE ILLVSTRIV

96. Lyons, in the sixteenth century, shown in a contemporary print.

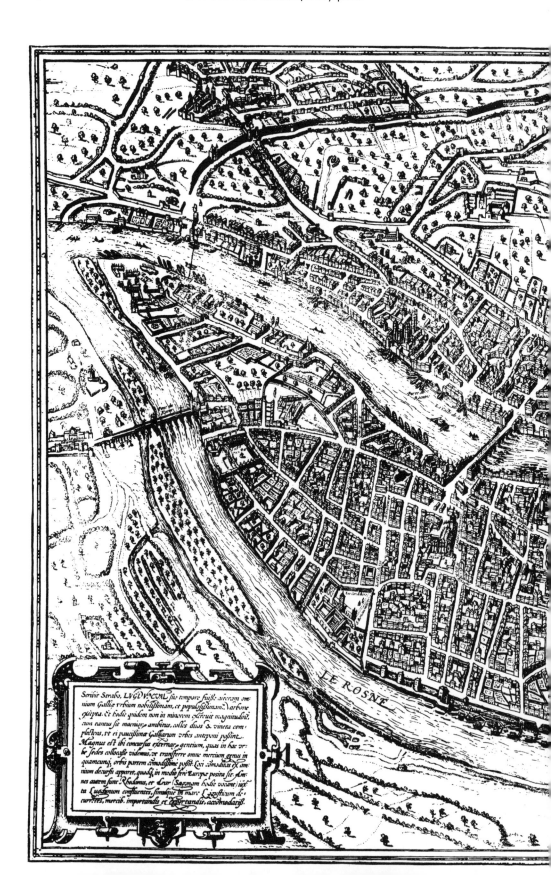

ONVM

Lÿon. Qui de la France
Sers de force & rempart,
Lÿon, qui de plaifance
Reluis de toute part.
La Riuiere du Rhosne
doucement decoulant
Qui embraſſe la Saone
Te rendent opulent.

MANTVA.

Mantua, Lombardiæ Transpada:
næ vrbs clarißima et antiquißima,
venustißimum, in medio paludium.
situm obtinet Anno salutis ꟾↃↃ
ꟾↃ LXXV. ad viuum delineata.

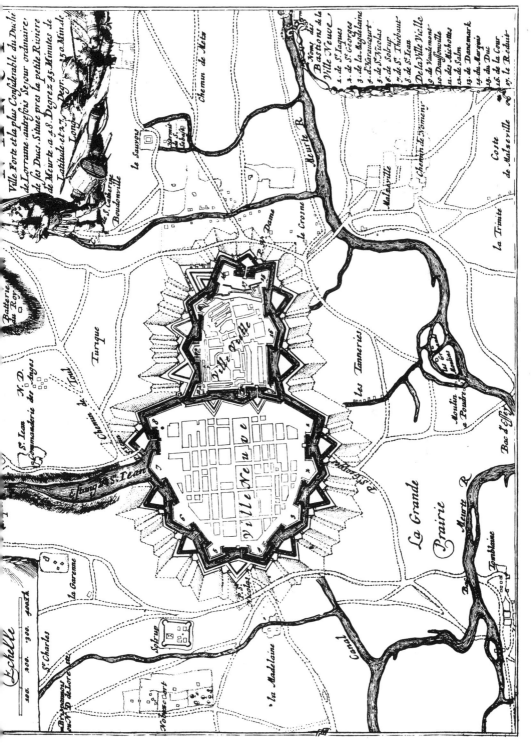

98. Nancy, perspective view, from De Fer, 1645. The enlargement of the city is clearly discernible.

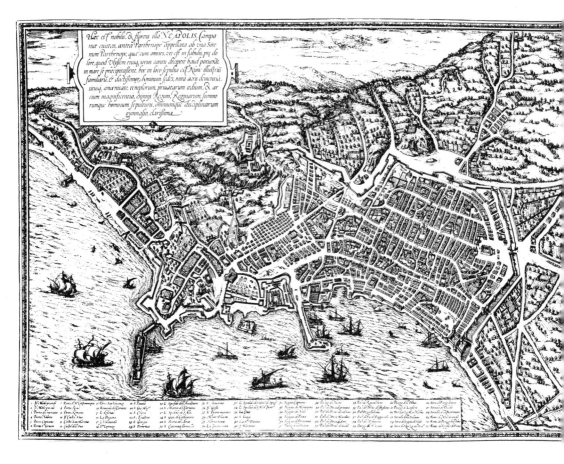

100. Palermo, perspective view, from Bertelli, 1599.
101. Palermo, airview of the Via Maqueda (vertical line) crossing the Via Toledo at Quattro Canti.

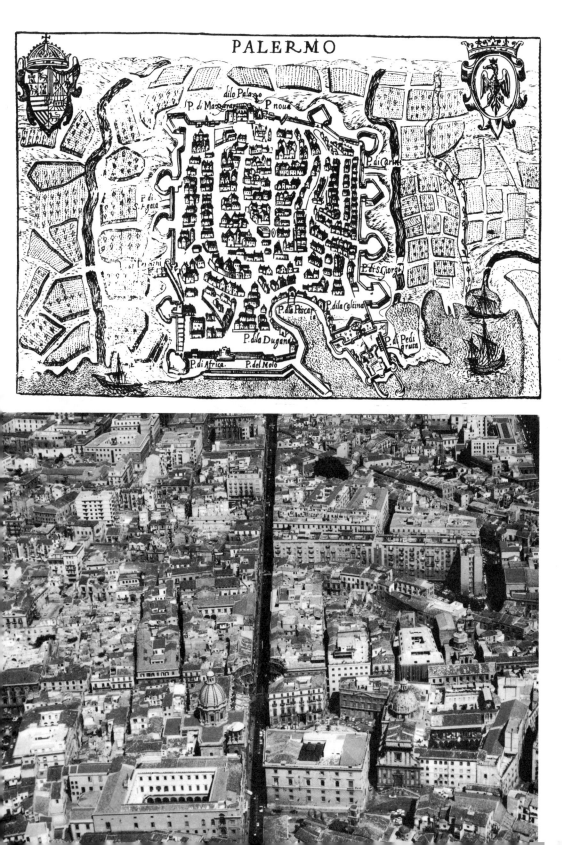

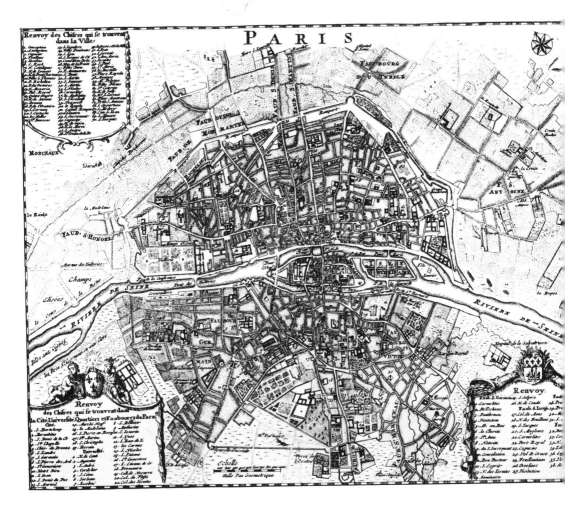

103. Paris, view of the Quay des Augustins and the Pont St.-Michel, print by Israel Silvestre, 1658.
104. Philippeville, plan, from De Fer, 1645.

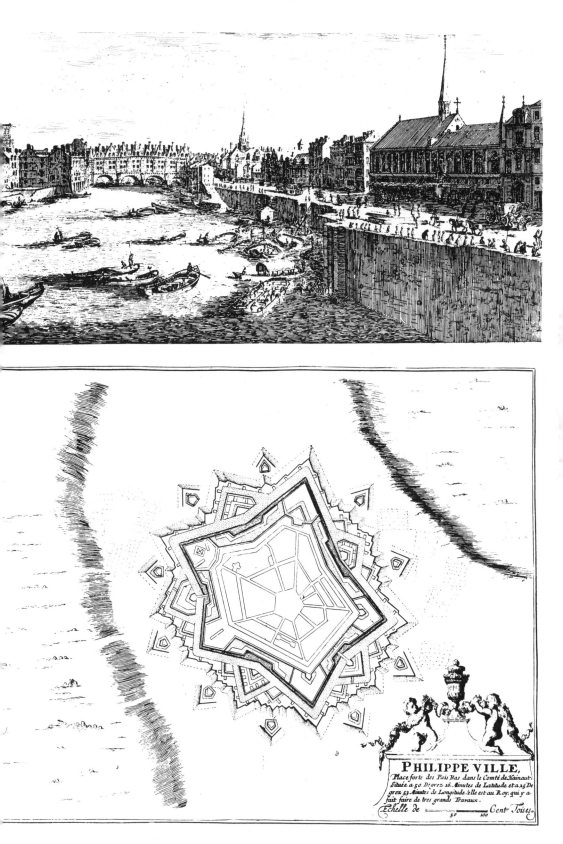

PHILIPPE VILLE,
Place forte des Pais Bas dans le Comté de Hainaut.
Située a 50 Degrez 16. Minutes de Latitude et a 25 Degrez 53 Minutes de Longitude. elle est au Roy, qui y a fait faire de tres grands Travaux.
Echelle de — 50 — 100 Cent Toises.

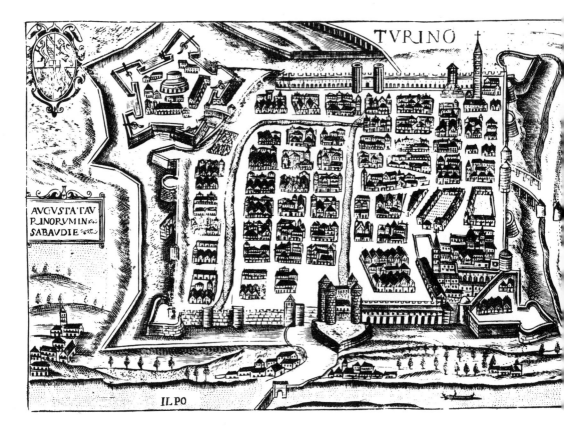

TVRINO

AVGVSTA TAV
RINORVM IN
SABAVDIE

IL PO

century, the different religious and political conditions were to impose a radical change on the program of Raphael and Bramante.

During his fifteen years of work in Rome, Bramante contributed in two ways to the development of the Renaissance concept of city planning: by putting the problem of the "monument" in new terms and by establishing the genre of the small palace (which was viewed no longer as an affirmation of prestige but as a city house, *Figs. 55a–b*). This new genre was developed by Raphael (1488–1520), Peruzzi (1481–1536), and Antonio da Sangallo (1455–1534) and had great influence on the noble residences of many Italian cities.

The perfect monument was the basilica of St. Peter's, which represented not only the spiritual authority of the Church, but the historical foundation of that authority as well (*Fig. 56*). Breaking completely with the form of the old basilica, a Latin cross, Bramante designed a centrally planned church in the form of a Greek cross (*Fig. 58*). Beyond the ideological and symbolic meaning associated with the central plans of the sacred buildings of the Renaissance (as demonstrated by Rudolf Wittkower in his *Architectural Principles in the Age of Humanism)*, the plan designed by Bramante, with its wings grafted onto a central, plastic nucleus, fitted into the space of the city with a constructive and articulate function. As the ideal center of universal space, the Christian "monument" tended to coordinate its plastic nucleus with the space of Rome in its role as the supreme historical and Christian city. The intention to have St. Peter's serve a primarily urbanistic function was shown by the need to insert it into the living dimension of the city even before it was built, and by the extension of one of the naves, intended to facilitate the passage of corteges and processions inside the church and thus to establish a continuity between the movement of the faithful both inside and outside the building.

Michelangelo (1475–1564), who took over the direction of the work after a considerable lapse, returned to the idea of absolute centrality, and actually strengthened this by tightening even more the mass around the dominating volume of the great dome (*Fig. 57*). A Florentine, he brought the urbanistic theme of Brunelleschi's dome of Santa Maria del Fiore to its ultimate consequence as the symbolic and characteristic form of a city, and in the case of Rome, of a city which in its turn represented the whole Christian world. Even today, in spite of the vast, chaotic expansion of Rome, the dome of St. Peter's is the characteristic element of the cityscape. It must be borne in mind that Rome's site, amid seven hills made views from above normal (*Fig. 54*). Precisely because a view from "ground level" was hardly significant, the city did not appear as a system of regular perspective layouts, but as a panorama or urban landscape, closely related to the natural landscape created by the Tiber and surrounding hills. In this setting Michelangelo's dome is dominant (*Fig. 59*).

The religious policies of the Counter Reformation were based on propaganda and on the worship of masses. Because of this it was felt necessary to give the "monument" of St. Peter's colossal dimensions, even beyond Michelangelo's "gigantism." Therefore, the plan for lengthening the nave was revised and the length extended. Carlo Maderno's works changed Michelangelo's plastic conception in an irreparable way but, in compensation, extended the body of the church into the city. St. Peter's was no longer a plastic block, weighty with symbolic meanings; it was a covered urban space, like the great public basilicas of ancient Rome (*Fig. 56*).

In the seventeenth century Bernini (1598–1680) was to recognize and accentuate this characteristic, both with his decorative emphasis on the interior space of the basilica, and especially in his great elliptical colonnade which took up the circular shape of the dome. The colonnade was simply the transformation, on a gigantic scale, of the ancient quadriporticus, which in early Christian basilicas was constructed as a useful and integral part of the building. It was, therefore, a part of the church which is transformed into a great square, linked to the rest of the city by a whole system of streets. The conceptions of Alberti and Rossellino had been turned around. They had extended the architectural form to the city. Now the architectural form had disintegrated, expressing itself in urban space.

The historical-ideological meanings of Rome were twofold, even if they were so closely linked that the second could be considered an extension of the first. Rome was not only the historical city par excellence, in whose appearance the idea of civic or national authority was realized; it was also the supreme Christian city in which the spiritual authority of the Church was reflected. Between the two phases there had been historical continuity—since the Church was born into the heart of the Roman Empire—and ideological continuity, because the Church based its canon on Roman law. Michelangelo expressed the religious symbolism in St. Peter's, and the civil and historical symbolism in the Piazza del Campidoglio (*Figs. 57–63*). The elements of city planning essential to his layout of the Piazza del Campidoglio were two: the concept of a plastically unified organism made up of three coordinated palaces, and the conception of the piazza no longer as a void between two perspective wings but as a solid plastic space with strong development of its articulated framework in the facades of the two side palaces. It should be noted that in the center of the piazza is the ancient statue of Marcus Aurelius, the Roman emperor who appeared as the precursor of the Christian conversion of Rome.

Beside these great urbanistic changes, a more modest, practical activity (but from the viewpoint of the development of city planning, no less important) was taking place in Rome, due in particular to Antonio de Sangallo the Younger. With an endless number of interventions, often only partial—of retouching and adapting—Sangallo contributed more than any other man to the restoration of the buildings in Rome. He was probably the first to realize that the appearance of a city did not depend only on the will of the prince and the genius of the great architect, but on the cultural level of the citizens and on the professional capacities of the technicians.

The city politics of the Renaissance popes were decided by the conditions of the city at the start of the fifteenth century: overcrowded quarters separated by vast uninhabited areas. Since the main cause of this disorder was the scarcity of water after the collapse of the Roman aqueducts, the most urgent problems were to ensure restoration of the water mains and to patch up the torn, split city network. Sixtus IV (pontificate, 1471–1484) was the first pope to pose the question of Roman social life. He built the Ponte Sisto to link up the populous quarter of Trastevere to the heart of the city, and so placed the great hospital of Santo Spirito in a nerve center of the city network. Julius II confirmed this link by opening the Via Giulia, which formed the chord of the bend in the Tiber and which, in the first half of the sixteenth century was the most elegant, vital street in the city (*Fig. 53*). Pius IV (pontificate, 1559–1565) opened the long Via Pia (*Fig. 64*), ending in the Porta Pia designed by Michelangelo. In the second part of the sixteenth century the Corso was planned as Rome's most vital artery.

The opening of these long and straight streets, linking up

distant quarters, was the first step toward the radical reform of city layout which took place under the pontificate of Sixtus V (pontificate, 1585–1590) with the plan of Domenico Fontana (1543–1607). The political plan of Sixtus V was farsighted: Rome was no longer merely the historical or holy city, it was the capital of the papal states, whose function was of major importance for the balance of power in Europe. It was an economically unproductive city (and Sixtus V tried, with little success, to remedy this problem also), but it was an international city, the center of diplomatic activities, the goal of travelers who came from all parts of Europe to obtain indulgences at the tombs of martyrs or to admire the ruins of antiquity.

Substantially, Fontana's plan consisted of an extension of the city limits beyond the Aurelian Walls to include the great early Christian basilicas, and to thin out the population crowded into the lower levels of the city by creating new quarters on higher grounds. The basic thrust of the program included: the reclamation of the marshy, unhealthy countryside; the repair of the consular roads to make access to the capital safer and easier; the installation of a water supply for the upper parts of the city to make them habitable (the Felice Aqueduct); and the opening of the great city streets. These streets connected the great basilicas in order to facilitate the passage of processions (*Figs. 65–67*); but the motives were social and economic as well as religious because the pilgrims, like the tourists today, were an essential element of the city's income. The "universal city" meant, on a practical level, "international city." The genius of Sixtus V lay in having understood that Rome was not so much the seat of a traditional community (which was both disjointed and inactive) as it was a city of people in transit—a crossroads and a reference point in the modern world.

Domenico Fontana had all the qualities needed to carry out the plan in the unexpectedly brief pontificate of Sixtus V, or, at least, to go so far that successors would be compelled to continue it (*Fig. 68*). He was more a technician in the modern sense of the word than a traditional artist; he knew how to establish a program which, apart from controlling the expansion of the city up to the time of its annexation by the Italian state, constituted, also in the aspect of visual space, the basis of the imposing character that Rome was to assume in the seventeenth century (*Figs. 69–71*). The principle of his plan was communication; long, wide, straight roads (for example, the Via delle

Quattro Fontane, which links Trinità dei Monti to Santa Maria Maggiore; *Fig. 66*) and wide squares for easier circulation of traffic. The buildings were by now merely walls of the streets, interminable facades with long rows of windows, all alike, almost without decoration or projecting elements. With Fontana, in fact, urbanism had discovered its modern instrument: that which is today called the *piano regolatore* (regulating plan).

## VENICE AND VICENZA

Venice could not expand very far. Hers was a flourishing, prosperous community enclosed within precise limits and laid out in a pattern almost impossible to change (*Fig. 72*). The network of canals and narrow streets was closely knit, irregular, and intricate; but these narrow, shadowy passages were compensated for by unexpectedly opening onto larger, light-filled spaces: the *campi* and *campielli*, the Grand Canal, the long trapezoid of the Piazza San Marco (*Fig. 74*). The urban horizon was low and indefinite: a lagoon, with its shifting transparencies of air and water (*Fig. 72*). In contrast, the architecture developed upward, with the bright colors of red bricks and cornices of white stone. As a perspective of planes and volumes was not possible, the city's space was characterized essentially by color.

In the second half of the sixteenth century the works of Andrea Palladio (1518–1580) marked a turning point in the concept of the size of urban space. The great architect from Padua was responsible for the churches of San Giorgio Maggiore (*Fig. 73*) and the Redentore and also for the incompleted project for rebuilding the Rialto Bridge along classical, monumental lines (*Figs. 73, 75*). The Rialto Bridge was the nexus of the city structure; it crossed the Grand Canal, linking the two sections of the city, and was also at the center of public life—the market. Palladio enhanced this traditional function of the bridge by locating seventy-two shops there, and with the use of solemn, classical forms he sought to underline and celebrate this most picturesque, vivid aspect of the common people.

The facades of Palladio's two churches were in keeping with classical concepts, but the structure and the movement of their mass aimed at obtaining maximum expanse of colored surfaces: the facades were white, reflecting the light, the curtain walls were pink, the dome pearl gray. One of the churches was on the island of San Giorgio; the other on the Giudecca. Both lay across the canal of San Marco and served as a backdrop to the view from the piazzetta, linked by the shape and color of their domes to the greatest Venetian basilica, San Marco. It was clear that the architect conceived of the two buildings in relation to the cityscape and to its essential color scheme; and by including the large mirror of the basin in the visual space of the city he increased the illusion of its size. Through these relationships, at a distance, natural space (in this case water and sky) became essential parts of the urban space.

The same thing occurred in Vicenza, the center of Palladio's activity. Vicenza was a city of Roman origin, and it is clear that Palladio intended to give the city an imaginary classical appearance. He transformed the old municipal palace into a Roman public basilica, and by adding superb facades, improved the palaces on both sides of the main street which followed the line of the ancient decumanus. The permanent stage set of the Teatro Olimpico, with its perspective streets, gave a clear idea of what the image of a classical city was to Palladio (*Fig. 76*). Even his palaces, furthermore, were planned in accordance with the perspective of the streets: Their architectural orders began above high plinths and the decorations became more elaborate higher up so as to create a greater play of light. There were always two viewpoints, both foreshortened: one along the line of the street and one frontal from below.

The austere city scenery had, however, another side to it, explained by the character and way of life of Vicenzan society, of which Palladio was a great interpreter. Vicenza formed part of the powerful Venetian Republic. Its aristocracy, with no political ambitions, had strong cultural interests which they demonstrated by creating a city of great nobility. In no other Italian city, in less than forty years, were so many illustrious palaces built. To place the elegant prospect of a palace along the principal streets was in a way a tribute that great families felt obliged to pay to the community. The ideal image of the city for Palladio was not theoretical but basically historical.

The life of the rich families of Vicenza was divided between the city and the countryside. During the long vacations when they administered their estates in the fertile hills around the city, their social life—the round of receptions, parties, and concerts—continued to be as active as it was in the city. For the same families for whom the austere palaces in the city were built, Palladio built pleasure villas in the country. Classical form, which implied a unitary concept of history and nature, was the common factor in Palladio's rural and urban architecture. It involved the same kind of "view from a distance" that he had used in Venice.

Palladian villas, even if they did not enter the same visual field, were an essential element of Vicenzan urbanism. They were also designed urbanistically, with plans that were freely articulated in the open space of the countryside, and with various units of the buildings clearly distinguished for the function they served: living quarters for the nobles and for the servants and various types of farm buildings (*Fig. 77*). In no other architect than Palladio did architectural morphology become of such value as a determinative element in city space. No other architect resolved the problem posed in the fifteenth century by Brunelleschi and Alberti with such clarity: the relationships between civilization (or history) and nature, between the urban nucleus of the city and the surrounding lands. The full resolution of these relationships, which came later, was due to the enormous influence of Palladio outside Italy, especially in England.

# RENAISSANCE NEW TOWNS

## LEGHORN

The idea of the value of the city, which began and was affirmed during the Renaissance, explains the *ex novo* rise of certain urban communities. Leghorn was born out of a strictly economic commercial interest; before the Medici bought it from Genoa in 1421, it was no more than a small Tyhrrenian landing place, a subsidiary of the nearby Pisan port (*Fig. 94*). In the sixteenth century, under Cosimo I and Ferdinand I of Tuscany, it was developed into an important commercial port with special privileges which made it, within a few years, one of the busiest ports in the Mediterranean. The Medici recognized the need to attach a city to the port so they "invented" one, even giving it a social content, granting privileges, and specially constructing houses for foreign merchants (especially Jews and Greeks) who settled there to trade. The city was built in a short space of time from plans drawn up in part by Bernardo Buontalenti (the finest Florentine architect of the second half of the sixteenth century) with a modern, star-shaped system of fortifications. The layout was regular: wide, broad straight streets, suitable for the heavy traffic, and with access to the docks of the Mediterranean port. There were no monumental perspectives, but the quality of the buildings was high, even though they were built for strictly functional purposes. At the close of the sixteenth century Leghorn was possibly the most modern city in Europe.

## SABBIONETA

Sabbioneta, near Mantua, on the other hand, was a typical cultural city. It was merely a small country village when Vespasiano Gonzaga (1531–1591) decided to make it an ideal city in the manner of the ancients. He gave it a rectangular street plan, oriented on the axis of the main street, which gave access to the two city gates and he fortified the polygonal perimeter. Gonzaga also proposed to give the city a content and a function; apart from great palaces he had built churches, schools, a library, a hospital, a mint, a huge Gallery of Antiquities, and the Teatro Olimpico (the work of Vincenzo Scamozzi, Palladio's great pupil) (*Figs. 78–79*). There was even a printing office famous for its excellent Hebrew editions. After the death of Vespasiano Gonzaga, the city declined culturally, reverted to being a rural village and today is partly in ruins. It was significant for the history of Renaissance culture, however, that humanistic studies were considered an urban function of such importance as to justify the creation of a new city.

## PALMANOVA

Palmanova, near Udine in Friuli, was a military city, a fortress and a permanent garrison protecting the northeast border of the Venetian Republic. As regards its layout Palmanova was the typical ideal city, the one which most clearly reflects the plans of theoreticians (*Figs. 80–81*). A theoretician actually worked there, the same Vincenzo Scamozzi (1522–1616) who had planned the theater of Sabbioneta in the Palladian manner. The perimeter of the city formed a complex defense system and was a model of fortification techniques at the close of the sixteenth century: radial roads leading from the polygonal ramparts to a hexagonal central square.

# CONCLUSION

The myth of the ideal city, born out of the humanistic thought of the early Renaissance, had two opposite results: On the one hand it led to the utopian theory of the perfect government, which created a flourishing literature right down to the eighteenth century; and on the other, it led to the military town, both fortress and barracks, of which we have numerous examples, especially in seventeenth- and eighteenth-century Germany. Although seemingly paradoxical, this is easily explained in that the ideal city always originated at the behest of an absolute ruler—a sovereign. It was founded on the desire for power; and the desire for power inevitably translates itself into the potential of war. Among the ideas developed in the urbanistic wing of Italian Renaissance culture, the concept of the ideal city is certainly the most abstract and also that which found most immediate acceptance outside Italy. The many towns which grew up in the second half of the sixteenth century, especially along the Imperial border with France, were all ideal military towns: fortresses and barracks.

However, the concept of city planning in the Renaissance was not that expressed in the theory of the ideal city, but that which was manifest in the actual transformation of ancient cities in keeping with a profound interpretation of history and the life of the community. This was not based on the enlightened Platonic ideology of power, but on the moral authority of living experience. This historicizing urbanism of the Italian Renaissance did not have immediate repercussions elsewhere in Europe, and, in fact, great European cities during the fifteenth and sixteenth centuries developed in a disorderly manner under the pressure of demographic or economic needs or, in certain cases, according to early land speculation. Only occasionally in the sixteenth century, under the impulse of social ideals connected with religious reform and the consequent developments of what could be called a paleo-industrial economy, did urban transformations, especially in Germany, reflect the need to improve the standard of living of the lower classes. A typical example is Augusta, where the great banking family, the Fuggers, in the first half of the century, had built a whole quarter of workers' houses laid out in rows and equipped for social services. But with the diffusion of classical culture, the concept of city planning worked out by Italian Renaissance architects became the essential basis for what was to be, throughout Europe, the social, political, and artistic character of the *capital city*, the city which represented the authority of the state and its moral and cultural force in the modern system of great European powers.

# APPENDIX:
# LIST OF CITIES WITH BIBLIOGRAPHIES

The following notes describe the principal urbanistic changes of European cities and towns which have some artistic interest and, where possible, provide a concise bibliography.

## AMSTERDAM

*Figs. 82–83.*

In the fifteenth century the medieval nucleus of Amsterdam was extended, first to the east, then to the west and south. The city had originally been surrounded by a system of defensive canals, but in 1481 it acquired a fortified wall with three city gates. A plan for further expansion to the east was drawn up at the end of the sixteenth century, incorporating the port in the new line of defense. The increase of population and the expansion of the city were related to the great development of maritime trade which began in 1585 when nearby Antwerp was taken over by Spain and the Schelde closed by the Estates General.

D'Ailly, A. E., et al., *Zeven eeuwen Amsterdam*, 6 vols., 1942–1950.
Kok, A. A., *De Historische Schoonheid van Amsterdam*, 1941.

## ANTWERP

*Figs. 84–85.*

The economic fortune of Antwerp rose in the fifteenth century when Bruges began to decline because of the gradual silting up of its harbor. The city grew rapidly in the sixteenth century under the patronage of Charles V: The population increased to 125,000, the harbor traffic flourished, and in 1562 Amsterdam became the seat of the Council of the Hanseatic League. The city declined after the siege of 1583, when it became a Spanish possession.

In the Middle Ages, Antwerp was little more than a village protected by a ditch (the record of which is preserved in the *rue du Fossé du Bourg*). In the sixteenth century the city was enlarged systematically following a series of plans. The most important was drawn up in 1507 and put into operation in 1542. The development of the city (which can be followed in the plans of Hieronimus Cock, of Virgilius Bononiensis, and of Cornelius Grapheus, preserved in the Plantin Museum) was largely carried out by Gilbert van Schoonbecke who worked for the municipality. Although he was not an artist, Van Schoonbecke may be considered the first expert in zoning and subdivisioning; wherever possible, he gave his layouts a geometric design, but his chief interests were economics and the rational division of the area. In the old city, the Hôtel de la Ville (1561–1565), the Bourse, and the corporation buildings, as well as the homes of the rich merchant middle-class were grouped around the Grand Place and the Groote Markt (Grain Market). The residential quarters had buildings of a fairly high quality, but these did not assume a monumental character. In the new city, to the north of the canals of L'Ancre and Vieux Lions, the layout was like a checkerboard; this was the industrial, working-class quarter (breweries). Because expansion, once it had gone beyond the original plan, tended to spread out past the city walls, van Schoonbecke decided to expand eastward, acquiring vast plots of land on the Malines Road. It is to be noted that in this quarter he decided on a widely spaced layout and houses of an almost rural appearance with gardens.

The bastioned fort, a model of the most modern techniques of fortification, was the work of Donato Boni Pellezuoli of Bergamo; the citadel was by Paciotto.

Deventer, J. van, *Atlas des villes de la Belgique au XVI siècle*, Brussels, 1884.

Hazewinkel, J. F., "Le développement d'Anvers," *Annales de géographie*, XXXV, 1926.

Marion, F., *Antwerpen*, Brussels, 1950.

Noppen, G., *Antwerpen. Koningen der Schelde*, Antwerp, 1930.

Parent, P., *L'Architecture dans les Pays-Bas Méridionaux*, Paris-Brussels, 1926.

## CAMBRIDGE

*Figs. 86–87.*

The specific character of this university city dates from the thirteenth century, when various religious orders (Franciscan, Dominican, Augustinian, and Carmelite) settled at Cambridge and initiated courses of advanced studies, soon made available to lay students. In order to house these students, who were not allowed to live in the religious communities, hostels were built, becoming in time colleges with individual statutes and rules. The colleges, founded and endowed by sovereigns or by private individuals, underwent great development in the fifteenth and sixteenth centuries. Each college consisted of various elements (chapel, library, housing for professors and students, a communal dining hall, and the like), separated by courtyards and gardens. The large number of these colleges and the wide extensions of land used to build on for cultivation had a great influence on the form of the city: The network was widely spaced, with vast green areas. For a long time education was the sole function of Cambridge and influenced the city's economy by favoring the development of book production.

Atkinson, T. D., *Cambridge Described and Illustrated*, Cambridge, 1897.

Clark, J. W., *Cambridge Historical and Picturesque*, London, 1890.

Stubbs, C. W., *Cambridge*, London, 1905.

## CARPI

This is a small city in Emilia, near Modena. There is a fourteenth-century castle belonging to the Pio, enlarged and modified in the sixteenth century, which is on a large porticoed square from which the cathedral also rises. This is the kind of union between the residence of the *signore* and the center of city life that Bramante had already effected at Vigevano in the last decade of the fifteenth century.

## CHARLEVILLE

Founded by Charles Gonzaga-Nevers, Duke of Rethel, as a military town, Charleville was built between 1606 and 1620 by Clement Métézeau. The fortified perimeter is star-shaped, the network of roads orthogonal. Despite the essentially strategic purpose of Charleville, there were perspective and townscape features of the Italian type in its architectural structure. The central square, known as the Place Ducale, was quite large and surrounded by arcades. The main streets ran into three corners of the square.

Hubert, J., *Histoire de Charleville*, Charleville, 1854.

## CIVITAVECCHIA

*Fig. 88.*
This ancient Roman port, dating from the time of Trajan (first century, A.D.), was rebuilt and enlarged in the sixteenth century by Pope Julius II and Pope Paul III in order to turn it into a coastal outlet for the papal states. The great fortress which protects the city was begun in 1508 by Bramante and continued by Antonio da Sangallo.

Galisse, C., *Storia di Civitavecchia*, Florence, 1898.

## CORSIGNANO

*See Pienza.*

## FERRARA

For the expansion of Ferrara ordered by Ercole d'Este and its planning by Biagio Rossetti (the most important urban enterprise of the fifteenth century) *see my discussion on pp. 31–33 and Figs. 48–52.*

Zevi, B., *Biagio Rossetti*, Turin, 1964. This is a complete critical study, accompanied by amply graphic and photographic documentation, on the transformation of Ferrara and on the work of Biagio Rossetti. It is a fundamental text, also from the methodological point of view, for the study of city planning in the Renaissance.

## FLORENCE

*See also my discussion on pp. 20, 23–29 and Figs. 17–18, 32–44.*
The first ring of walls dates from the eleventh century, the second from the twelfth century, and the third from the time of Dante. This last was the period of the flowering of the city and of rapid increase in population. During the fifteenth and sixteenth centuries, changes in the city layout were limited to minor rearrangements. The extreme importance of Florence's contribution to Renaissance city planning cannot be

demonstrated by actual planning but by the decisive works of her architects. It must also be remembered that for Alberti and Brunelleschi, city planning was viewed in terms of three-dimensional design on a given site rather than on paper plans. Besides the dome of the Duomo, the buildings which contributed most in the fifteenth century to the creation of an urban atmosphere were the *Ospedale degli Innocenti* by Brunelleschi, which served as a beginning for the construction of the porticoed Piazza dell'Annunziata (*Fig. 40*), and his two churches, San Lorenzo and Santo Spirito; the facade of Santa Maria Novella by Alberti, which gave a new character to the preexisting square (*Fig. 44*); the Dominican convent of San Marco by Michelozzo (which contained the prime example of a Renaissance library); the Palazzo Pitti after a design by Brunelleschi (*Fig. 41*); the Palazzo Medici-Riccardi by Michelozzo: the Palazzo Rucellai by Alberti (*Fig. 47*); and the Palazzo Strozzi by Benedetto da Maiano and Giuliano da Sangallo.

In the sixteenth century, Cosimo I ordered Giorgio Vasari (1511–1574) to build a palace for the city's administrative and judiciary offices (the Uffizi). By freely interpreting a Michelangelesque theme, Vasari planned two long porticoed facades along opposite sides of a very narrow square—almost a street (*Fig. 42*). The focal point at one end was a portico giving onto the Lungarno, and at the other, it was the jutting corner and the tower of the Palazzo della Signoria (now the Palazzo Vecchio). Instead of carving out a delicately beautiful place in the city layout with a huge palace, he split the building into two parallel structures and linked the Piazza della Signoria to the natural generating element of the city, the river Arno. In this way, he interpreted the architectural form of the palace within the context of city planning and ingeniously so. Another structure which was dictated in every detail by the nature of the urban tableau was the sixteenth-century Ponte Santa Trinità by Bartolomeo Ammanati (1511–1592). The bridge was constructed in a series of rhythmic curves, beginning with the curve of the parapet that linked the distant line of the horizon to the curves of the arches, which gradually narrowed down to sink into the sharply pointed piers which cut the current (*Fig. 43*). The Ponte Santa Trinità was destroyed by the Germans in 1944, but was accurately reconstructed after the war.

Biadi, L., *Notizie storiche sulle antiche fabbriche di Firenze*, Florence, 1824.

Malespini, R., *Storia antica della edificazione di Firenza ...*, Florence, Giunti ed., 1598.

Reumont, A., *Tavole cronologiche e sincrone della storia fiorentina*, Florence, 1851.

Ross, I., *Florentine Palaces*, London, 1900.

## GENEVA

*Fig. 89.*

The great flowering of Geneva ended in 1463 when Louis XI transferred the fairs which had been held in Champagne to Lyons. During the religious wars of the sixteenth century, the city was isolated and forced to abandon her five suburbs, bringing the inhabitants inside the city walls. The increase of population was aggravated by the arrival of French Protestant refugees. This increase in population density within fixed boundaries led to maximum exploitation of the land and to the adoption of tall buildings (five to six stories high).

Blondel, L., "Le developpement urbain de Genève à travers les siècles," *Cahiers de Préhistoire et d'Archéolpgie.*
Patio, G., *Genève à travers les siècles*, Geneva, 1900.

## GENOA

*Figs. 90–91.*
The old, closely packed aggregate of Genoa remained unchanged until about the middle of the sixteenth century when, because of the recently achieved political and economic stability, there was an intensive wave of building. The Genoese nobility moved to the higher part of the city, where they built lavish palaces with terraced gardens on the mountain slopes. The chief innovations were construction of the Piazza delle Fontane Marose and, in particular, the carefully planned opening of the Via Aurea (later known as the Via Nuova and now as the Via Garibaldi) in 1550. The monumental character of this street was achieved largely by the architecture of Galeazzo Alessi (1512–1572), with the Cambiaso and Lercari palaces, and of R. Lurago with the Doria, Podestà, and Imperiale palaces.

De Negri, E., *Galeazzo Alessi, architetto a Genova*, Genoa, 1958.
*Genova, Strada Nuova*, edited by the University of Genoa (Instituto di Architettura e Rilievo dei Monumenti), Genoa, 1967. This is a complete critical study, accompanied by ample graphic, photographic, and bibliographic documentation on the planning and development of the "patrician" street in sixteenth-century Genoa.

## GUASTALLA

This small, fortified town between Reggio Emilia and Mantua belonged to a branch of the Gonzaga family in the second half of the fifteenth century. The town, protected by ditches and cortine walls with seven bastions, had a rectilinear layout based on two almost parallel roads running from north to south. The roads were out of line with the axis of the two city gates to facilitate defense. Ferrante Gonzaga, who acquired Guastalla in 1539, gave over its enlargement and fortification to the architect Domenico Giunti of Lodi; after 1567 the work was continued by Cesare Gonzaga. The town plan of Guastalla inspired that of Sabbioneta (see below), built at the order of Vespasiano Gonzaga and carried out in a few decades in more uniform manner.

Affo, I., *Istoria della città e ducato di Guastalla*, Guastalla, 1785–1787.
Venamati, G. B., *Istoria della città di Guastalla*, Parma, 1674.

## LE HAVRE

*Fig. 92.*

The founding of this port city was planned in 1515 by the chief citizens of Rouen because of the gradual silting up of the port of Honfleur. Cyron Le Roy was put in charge of the work, and, realizing that the port would inevitably lead to a city, he speculated in land beside the docks (part of the quarter of Nôtre Dame). In 1541 Francis I recognized the possibilities of developing the port and employed the military architect Girolamo Bellarmati (1490–1555) to "build a city with a port, beautiful houses and fortifications following the chosen plan." The first enlargement of the original nucleus was to the east, creating the quarter of San Francisco. Afterward the city continued to expand solely from intense exploitation of the land.

Herval, R., *Un ingénieur sienois en France au XVI siècle*, 1960.

Marcellais, G., *Mémoires de la fondation et origine de la ville Françoise de Grâce*, Le Havre, 1847.

Martin, A., *Origins du Havre—Description historique et topographique de la ville Française et du Havre du Grâce*, Fecamps, 1885.

Morbent, J., *Le Havre ancien et moderne, et ses environs*, Le Havre, 1825.

Nerval, S. de., *Documents relatifs à la fondation du Havre*, 1875.

## HESDIN

*Fig. 93.*

Hesdin is a type of fortress city, built by Charles V, on the plan of the military architect Sebastiano van Noyen, to protect the Artois frontier. The town replaced another which had been conquered and razed in 1553. The polygonal plan contained nine *insulae*, with the marketplace in the center; a river runs through it. In 1593, during the reign of Philip II, Hesdin was enlarged to the north with the addition of a radially planned quarter.

Allent, A., *Histoire du corps impérial du Gènie*, Paris, 1805.

Lion, J., *Hesdinfort*, Amiens, 1844.

Neunier, P., *Histoire d'Hesdin*, Montreuil, 1896.

## LEGHORN

*See also my discussion on p. 104 and Fig. 94.*

Leghorn is the first example of a port originally built and developed according to precise plans drawn up with its function in mind. Until the beginning of the sixteenth century, it was only a secondary staging area, almost a side branch of the nearby port for Pisa. Because of the progressive silting up of the latter, among other reasons, Cosimo I de'Medici decided to transform Leghorn into a great commercial port. He organized the defensive system and assisted its settlement by granting tax exemptions to foreign merchants who settled in the city. The urban population, not even 1,000 by 1560, grew to more than 8,000 just fifty years later. A study of the enlargement of the fortress and the city was ordered in 1576 by Grand Duke Francesco II, to be carried out by the architect Bernardo Buontalenti (c. 1536–1608). The plan called for a large number of middle-class dwellings to attract permanent immigrants. All streets led to the port, and were wide and straight to ease the transport of merchandise. The construction of the residential quarter was carried out under Ferdinando I according to the plans of Cogorano, since Buontalenti's plan had already been declared inadequate. In 1606 Leghorn achieved the status of a city. For Buontalenti's work see also Terra del Sole.

Baruchello, M., *Livorno e il suo porto*, Leghorn, 1832.
Guarniéré, G., *Origine e sviluppo del porto di Livorno*, Leghorn, 1911.
Piombanti, G., *Guida di Livorno*, Leghorn, 1903.

## LORETO

*Fig. 95.*

The center of a cult and the goal of pilgrims, Loreto is a typical example of an urban aggregation clustered around a religious monument. The Sanctuary was founded in 1468 by Pope Paul II on the site where, according to legend, the home of the Virgin Mary in Nazareth had been miraculously transported. The cult of the Madonna of Loreto was encouraged by the Catholic Church in its struggle against the Protestants, who denied the divinity of the Virgin. In the sixteenth century the Sanctuary assumed the dimensions and importance of a great monument and was fortified, not only to protect its treasures, but also to symbolize its significance as a fortress of the faith.

Dal Monte, F., *Loreto e le sue difese militari*, Recanati, 1919.
Facco de Lagarda, E., *Loreto*, Rome, 1895.
Faurax, J., *Bibliographie Lorétaine*, Paris, 1913.
Pisani Dossi, G., *Guida della città di Loreto*, Siena, 1895.

## LYONS

*Fig. 96.*

The prosperity of the city began at the close of the fifteenth century, and reached a peak in the second half of the sixteenth century when the silk industry developed there. During this period Lyons became one of the most brilliant intellectual centers in France because of the presence of Marguerite of Navarre, the sister of the King.

In the Renaissance the city, which had been clustered at the foot of the Fourvière hill, expanded rapidly in the wide area between the Roanne and the Saône rivers. The city grew without a program, under the pressure of land speculation. Population density was high, the streets were narrow, and houses were built upward. The squares, which were laid out to give breathing space to the closely packed city (*Des Jacobins*, 1556; *Des Cordeliers*, 1557), were made possible by the clearing of cemeteries situated around churches. A more controlled development only began in 1562 when the Protestant Baron Des Adrets studied a defensive plan of importance to the city's topography. The modern

Place Bellecourt, used for military drills, was built by Des Adrets on lands confiscated from a convent. In 1560, he built a bridge over the Roanne which proved vital to the life of the city.

Montfalcon, G. B., *Le guide du voyageur et de l'amateur à Lyon*, Lyon, 1826.
René, J., *Lyon*, Paris, 1960.

## MANTUA

*Fig. 97.*
The old city was square and divided into districts. The oldest nucleus corresponded to the quarter of St. Peter. Besides the intervention of Leon Battista Alberti who built the monumental churches of Sant' Andrea and San Sebastiano, in the fifteenth and sixteenth centuries the chief urbanistic contributions to Mantua (due in particular to Gian-francesco and Ludovico Gonzaga) were the reclamation of marshy lands for city expansion, and the reordering of the city center by the articulated linking of the three piazzas of Erbe, Broletto, and Sordello.

Davari, S., *Notizie storiche-topografiche della città di Mantova*, Mantua, 1903.
Quazza, R., *Mantova attraverso i secoli*, Mantua, 1933.
Restori, U., *Mantova e dintorni*, Mantua, 1915.
Visi, G. B., *Notizie storiche della città e dello Stato di Mantova*, Mantua, 1782.

## NANCY

*Fig. 98.*
Italian influence could already be seen by the sixteenth century when nobles' residences were built around the ducal palace in the old town, although its layout remained medieval. The expansion of Nancy, the capital of Lorraine, due to the political and economic fortune of the city, soon made the ancient, turreted city wall inadequate. The new system of bastioned fortifications was built by the Sienese Girolamo Bellarmati, a military engineer in the service of the King of France since 1534 (see also Le Havre). At the end of the sixteenth century Charles IV of Lorraine decided on a further enlargement, doubling the area of the city. The plan of the new city within the polygonal fortified walls was drawn up by Girolamo Citoni on a regular checkerboard pattern.

Bergeret, A., *Nancy monumentale et pittoresque*, Nancy, 1897.
Hallays, A., *Nancy*, Paris, n.d.
Pfister, C., *Histoire de Nancy*, Paris, 1903–1908.

## NAPLES

*Fig. 99.*
The plan to renew and enlarge the city was conceived by Alfonso II of Aragon, and is described in a letter by Summonte as follows:
> *Erat illi in animo fluvium et longiquo per magnos acquaeductus in urbem ducere;* and, on completion of the great walls of the

city, which are now almost finished, all the principal roads of the city will be extended in a straight line, from wall to wall, removing all the uneven porticoes, corners and humps, and so all the streets from one end of the city to the other will be extended crossways, also in straight lines. In this way, both through the straightness of the streets and roads, and also through the natural sloping of the city from north to south, apart from the beauty of its equal units', this city will become the most elegant, clean city [*aliarum pace dixerim*] in all Europe, and will be polished as clean as a plate of burnished silver even after the slightest rainfall. And beyond this, once particular houses have their fountains, other fountains and public drinking places will be built at crossroads and suitable places, from which water may be spread over the streets when they have been swept in summer, so as to keep the ground free from dust and clean. Moreover, he desires to build a sumptuous temple, where the remains may be placed of all the Aragon progeny who die here. There will also be a great palace, near the Castello Novo, in the Piazza della Coronata, in which all the courts of justice will be arranged in diverse rooms, so that businessmen need not go to different places, but may carry out any business whatsoever, without suffering from the rain or the sun, and without tiring their bodies by hurrying from place to place.

This was the most important document of Renaissance city planning, understood as an agent of government. It was clearly related to Alberti's concepts, as proved by the reference to the beauty of a regular layout (equalità) and to the importance of a monument which was to be at the same time both church and mausoleum of the ruling family. The letter was first published in its entirety by Fausto Nicolini in *L'Arte napoletana del Rinascimento*, 1925.

Among the chief city-planning undertakings in Naples in the sixteenth century was the opening of the Via Toledo (now the Via Roma), commissioned by the Viceroy, Pedro de Toledo, to join the old city to the new quarters which were growing up on the eastern slopes of the Castel dell'Elmo. At the close of the century Domenico Fontana planned the road which runs along the seafront, and enlarged the Via Santa Lucia. He also built the enormous Palazzo Reale facing the bay.

Gothein, E., *Rinascimento nell'Italia Meridionale*, Florence, 1925.
Pane, R., *Architettura del Rinascimento in Napoli*, 1937.

## PALERMO

*Fig. 100–101.*

In the second half of the sixteenth century, under Spanish domination, the city was improved by filling in the two rivers which ran through it and turning them into roads. The most ancient axial street of the city (the Via del Cassero, now Via Toledo) was lengthened and straightened between 1564 and 1581. In 1597 another axis was opened, perpendicular to the first (Via Maqueda). The junction of the two roads (Quattro Canti) with fountains at the corners, repeated the motif of the Via delle Quattro Fontane in Rome.

Giovanni, V. di, *La topografia antica di Palermo*, Palermo, 1884.
Matteo, G. di, *Palermo nei secoli*. Palermo, 1958.
Pirrone, G., "Palermo; la sua storia e i suoi problemi," *Urbanistica*, VI, 1950.

## PALMANOVA

*See also my discussion on p. 105 and Figs. 80–81.*

Like Sabbioneta (see below), Palmanova, near Udine, is a completely new town (1598) built in a short time, following a unified, geometric plan. It was created with a specific aim in mind: to defend the eastern frontier of the Republic of Venice. The system of fortifications determined the shape of the city—a nine-pointed star, forming a polygon of eighteen sides. In the center is the hexagonal square from which the six main streets radiate.

Rosenfeld, L., *Palmanova*, Udine, 1888.
Savorgnan, F. B., "Palmanova eil suo ideatore Giulio Savorgnan," *Memorie storiche forogiuliesi*, XLVI, 1965.

## PARIS

*Figs. 102–103.*

At the beginning of the fifteenth century the urban character of Paris was already well defined. The Île de la Cité in the Seine was the original nucleus of the city, with the Cathedral of Nôtre Dame and the Palais Royale; the bridges of Nôtre-Dame and Saint-Michel joined the Cité to the opposite banks. The left bank had served, and still does, a primarily cultural function sharing the university, schools, and monasteries. The right bank was primarily commercial; the Hôtel de Ville and the markets (Les Halles) were built there. The town council controlled the development of Paris. Only in 1550 did the King show an interest in the city, although he still did not reside there. Henry II commissioned the Sienese Bellarmati to draw up a plan that would incorporate the quarter of St.-Germain within the city area (see also Le Havre and Nancy). In 1559, Henry IV transferred the royal residence to Paris and started the reordering of the Louvre. Later urban changes, especially in the seventeenth century, were to make of Paris the greatest capital in Europe.

Barbelou, J. P., *Demeures parisiennes sous Henri IV et Louis XIII*, Paris, 1965.
Berty, A., and L. M. Tisserand, *Topographie historique du vieux Paris*, Paris, 1887.
Franklin, *Les anciens plans de Paris*, 1752.
Jaillot, *Recherches critiques et topographiques sur la ville de Paris*, 1772.
Morizot, A., *Du vieux Paris au Paris moderne*, Paris, 1932.

## PHILIPPEVILLE

*Fig. 104.*

This was a fortress city founded by Charles V in 1555 to protect the frontier of the Holy Roman Empire and was then called Philippeville in honor of Philip II. The plan was drawn up by Sebastiano van Noyen (see also Hesdin). The fortified perimeter had five sides around a rectangular central square. The street network consisted of ten radial streets crossed by a system of concentric rings.

Borgnet, J., in *Annales de la Société d'Archéologie*, Namur, IX, 1865.
Robaulz, A. de., *Ibid.*, VI, 1860.

## PIENZA (CORSIGNANO)

*See my discussion on pp. 30–31 and Figs. 22–24.*

Carli, E., *Pienza*, 1965.

## PORTOFERRAIO

After Charles V had ceded this little coastal settlement, Cosimo I de' Medici transformed it into a fortified city against the invasions of Saracen corsairs. The plans were drawn up by the ducal architect, G. B. Bellucci, who was succeeded by G. B. Camerini. The residential quarter on the hillside follows a rectangular plan with slight deviations caused by the sloping of the ground. Near the port is the Piazza della Gran Guardia of elongated shape, and further inland, the Piazza d'Arme, which is rectangular. The streets radiating from the latter square are stepped because of the incline.

Foresi, *L'Elba illustrata*, Portoferraio, 1929.
Lambardi, S., *Memorie antiche e moderne dell'Isola dell'Elba*, Florence, 1791.
Mellini, V., *Memorie storiche dell'Isola d'Elba*, Florence, 1965.
Ninci, G., *Storia dell'Isola d'Elba*, Portoferraio, 1814.

## ROME

*See my discussion on pp. 32, 97–104 and Figs. 30–31, 53–71.*

## SABBIONETA

*See also my discussion on p. 104 and Figs. 78–79.*

Although it has now declined into a modest rural town, Sabbioneta retains the form that Vespasiano Gonzaga gave it. It has a star-shaped perimeter which encloses a regular layout of straight streets with two gates near each end of the central thoroughfare. Sabbioneta, with Palma-nova, is the actual realization of an ideal city. Vincenzo Scamozzi collaborated in planning it and constructed the theater on ancient lines (1590) following the example of Palladio's Teatro Olimpico (where Scamozzi himself had supervised the building). The calculated balance between military, civil, and cultural functions shows that Vespasiano Gonzaga was the first to think of city planning as an art of government.

Buzzi, P., *Dedalo*, VIII (1927–28), IX (1928–29).
Forster, K. W., "From 'Rocca' to 'Civitas': Urban Planning at Sabbioneta," *l'Arte*, fasc. 5 (March, 1969).
Intra, G. B., *Sabbioneta*, Mantua, 1909.
Marini, S., *Sabbioneta*, Casalmaggiore, 1914.
Racheli, A., *Memorie storiche di Sabbioneta*, Casalmaggiore, 1849.

## TERRA DEL SOLE

This was a fortified city on the Romagna border, founded by Cosimo I, Grand Duke of Tuscany, and designed by Buontalenti (see also Leghorn). The plan was orthogonal with the main axis linking the two city gates. The bastionated wall was a model of fortification technique.

Morini, M., "Terra del Sole e l'opera di Bernardo Buontalenti," *Atti del V Convegno Nazionale di storia dell'architettura*, Perugia, 1948.

## TURIN

*Fig. 105.*

The most ancient nucleus of Turin has always preserved its layout of the Roman city in the form of a gridiron, with great axial streets of the *cardo* and the *decumanus*. The city only began to grow larger in the second half of the sixteenth century, developing further the geometric Roman plan in a regular manner. Emanuele Filiberto di Savoia had new fortifications built, entrusting the project of the citadel to F. Paciotto (1563). Carlo Emanuele I ordered an architect from Orvieto, Ascanio Vittozzi, to enlarge the city to the south (Piazza Castello) and to the east (Via Nuova, now Via Roma). The architect Carlo di Castellamonte drew up the plan for the great Piazza S. Carlo which is enclosed by porticos, and also for the extension of the Via Nuova beyond the square. The main enlargements were carried out in the seventeenth and eighteenth centuries, continuing to extend the orthogonal layout of the ancient city.

Boggio, C., *Gli architetti Carlo e Amedeo di Castellamonte e lo sviluppo edilizio di Torino*, Turin, 1896.
Brinckmann, A. E., *Novum Theatrum Pedemonti*, Dusseldorf, 1931.
Carboneri, N., *Ascanio Vittozzi*, Rome, 1966.
Istituto di Architettura tecnica del Politecnico, *Forma urbana ed architettura nella Torino Barocca*, III, Unione tipografico-editrice torinese, 1968.
Toesca, P., *Torino*, Bergamo, 1911.

## URBINO

*See my discussion on p. 21 and Figs. 19–20.*

## VENICE

*See my discussion on pp. 101, 102 and Figs. 72–75.*

## VICENZA

*See my discussion on pp. 101–103 and Fig. 76.*

## VITRY-LE-FRANÇOIS

This fortified city was built by Francis I (reigned, 1515–1547) to defend the line of the Marne and the road to Paris. The plan, drawn up by the Bolognese Girolamo Marini in 1545, had a square shape with a rectangular network of roads. The town was destroyed during World War II.

Abbé Boitel, *Histoire de l'ancien et du nouveau Vitry*, Châlons, 1841.
Campana, C., *Vita del catholico ed invittissimo re don Filippo II*, Vicenza, 1605.

# BIBLIOGRAPHY

For an exposition and general treatment of the question of the Renaissance city, one always refers to the fundamental works of Pierre Lavedan (*Histoire de l'Urbanisme*, vol. III, Paris, 1941), Lewis Mumford (*The Culture of Cities*, New York, 1938, and *The City in History*, New York, 1961), Marcel Poëte (*Introduction à l'Urbanisme*, Paris, c. 1929), and Sigfried Giedion (*Space, Time and Architecture*, Cambridge, Mass., 1941). In addition, there are the recent volumes by Leonardo Benevolo (*Storia dell'architettura del Rinascimento*, Bari, 1968), which consider the evolution of architectural forms in relation to urban spaces. Since in the Renaissance the city came to be seen as a historical creation expressed in architectural-sculptural terms, general treatments of architectural history (such as Nikolaus Pevsner's model *An Outline of European Architecture*, London, 1945) are valuable in the study of city planning. Some studies devoted to a particular problem—in spite of their monographic character—take on methodological importance that goes beyond their specific argument: for example, Bruno Zevi's *Biagio Rossetti e la trasformazione urbanistica di Ferrara* (Turin, 1960) and Giorgio Simoncini's *Gli Architetti nella cultura del Rinascimento* (Bologna, 1967). One may also consult the article "Urbanistica" by Astegno in the *Enciclopedia Universale dell'arte*.

The following bibliography is divided into five categories: 1. Sources; 2. general works; 3. books on the architectural history of regions; 4. monographs on architects relevant to urban problems of the period; 5. essays on specific problems related to city planning. In each group, the references are listed in chronological order.

## SOURCES

Vitruvius. *De Architectura Libri decem.*

Alberti, Leon Battista. *De re aedificatoria.* P. Portoghesi, ed. Milan, 1966.

Filarete Antonio Averlino. "Trattato di architettura," *Eitelberger-Ilg's Quellenschriften*, Vol. III, W. V. Oettingen, ed. Vienna, 1890.

Colonna, Fra Francesco. *Hypnerotomachia Poliphili.* Aldo Manuzio, ed. Venice 1499.

Giorgio, Francesco di. *Trattati di architettura, ingegneria e arte militare.* C. Maltese, ed. Milan, 1967.

da Vinci, Leonardo. *Scritti.* J. Recupero, ed. Rome, 1966.

Serlio, Sebastiano. *I sette libri dell'architettura.* Venice, 1537–1557.

―――. *Sesto libro delle habitationi di tutti li gradi degli homini.* M. Rosci, ed. Milan, 1966.

Vignola, Jacopo Barozzi da. *Regole delle cinque ordini d'architettura.* Rome, 1562.

Palladio, Andrea. *I quattro libri d'architettura.* Venice, 1570.

Scamozzi, Vincenzo. *Dell'idea dell'architettura universale.* Venice, 1615.

Bellucci, G. B. (Sammarino). *Nuova inventione di fabricar fortezze di varie forme.* Venice, 1598.

122

# GENERAL WORKS

Strack, H. *Central-und Kuppelkirchen des Renaissance in Italien*. Berlin, 1882.

Frankl, P. *Die Renaissance Architektur in Italien*. Leipzig, 1912.

Gotch, J. A. *Early Renaissance Architecture in England*. London, 1914.

Willich, H. and Zucker, P. *Die Baukunst der Renaissance in Italien*. Potsdam, 1914.

Baum, J. *Baukunst und dekorative Plastik der Frührenaissance in Italien*. Stuttgart, 1920.

Frey, D. *Architettura della Rinascenza*. Rome, 1924.

Haupt, A. *Renaissance Palaces of Northern Italy and Tuscany*. London, 1931.

Giovannoni, G. *Saggi sull'architettura del Rinascimento*. Milan, 1931.

Piccinato, L. *L'urbanistica dell'antichità ad oggi*. Rome, 1943.

Weber, M. *City*. New York.

Whinney, M. *Renaissance Architecture in England*. London, 1952.

Wittkower, R. *Architectural Principles in the Age of Humanism*. London, 1952, and New York, 1965.

Rosenau, H. *The ideal city in its architectural evolution*. London, 1959.

Lugli, P. M. *Storia e culture della città italiana*. Bari, 1967.

## CITIES AND REGIONS

CAMPANIA. Pane, R. *L'architettura del Rinascimento a Napoli*. Naples, 1935; Hamberg, G. "Vitruvius, Fra Giocondo and the City Plan of Naples," *Acta Archaeologica*, Vol. XXXVI, 1965.

EMILIA. Malaguzzi-Valeri, F. *L'architettura a Bologna nel Rinascimento*. 1899; Raule, A. *L'architettura bolognese*. Bologna, 1952.

LATIUM. Zocca, M. "Sistemazioni urbanistiche del Rinascimento nel Lazio," in *Palladio*, 1943; Forster, O. M. "Bramantes erste Jahre in Rom," *Wallraf-Richartz Jahrbuch*, Vol. XV, 1953; Magnuson, T. *Studies in Roman Quattrocento Architecture*. Stockholm, 1958.

LOMBARDY. Terrasse, G. *L'architecture lombarde de la Renaissance (1450–1515)*. Paris, 1926; Salmi, M. "Antonio Filarete e l'architettura lombarda del primo Rinascimento," *Atti del primo Congresso Nazionale di Stora dell'architettura*. Florence, 1936.

PIEDMONT. Cavallari-Murat, A. *Breve storia dell'urbanistica in Piemonte*. Turin, 1960.

TUSCANY. Steigmann, C. and von Geymüller, H. *Die Architektur der Renaissance in Toskana*. Munich, 1909; Patzak, B. *Palast und Villa in Toskana*. Leipzig, 1912–1913; Paatz, W. and B. *Die Kirchen von Florenz*. Frankfurt, 1940–54.

VENETO. Paoletti, P. *L'architettura e la scultura del Rinascimento a Venezia*. Venice, 1897.

## MONOGRAPHS

*Bramante*, by O. M. Forster (Vienna, 1956).

*Filippo Brunelleschi*, by G. C. Argan (Milan, 1955).

*Brunelleschi e Michelozzo*, by L. Gori-Montanelli (Florence, 1957).

*Die Architekturtheorie des Filarete*, by P. Tigler (Berlin, 1963).

*Francesco di Giorgio*, by R. Papini (Florence, 1946).
*Leonardo da Vinci*, by L. H. Heydenreich (Basel, 1953).
*L'Urbanistica negli studi di Leonardo da Vinci*, by E. Sisi (Florence, 1953).
*The Architecture of Michelangelo*, by J. Ackerman (London, 1960).
*Andrea Palladio*, by R. Pane (Turin, 1948).
*Raffaello*, by R. Salvini (Milan, 1961).
*Biagio Rossetti*, by B. Zevi (Turin, 1960).
*Giuliano da Sangallo*, by G. Marchini (Florence, 1942).

## ESSAYS

Heydenreich, L. H. "Pius II als Bauherr von Pienza," *Zeitschrift für Kunstgeschichte*, Vol. VI, 1937.

Argan, G. C. "Urbanistica e Architettura," *Le Arti*, 1939.

Zocca, M. "Origini ed evoluzione degli schemi urbanistici," *Palladio*, 1953.

De La Croix, H. "Military architecture and the radial city plan in the sixteenth century," *Art Bulletin*, 1960.

Buttafava, C. *Visioni di città nelle opere d'arte del Medioevo e del Rinascimento*. Milan, 1963.

Ackerman, J. "Sources of the Renaissance Villa," *Studies in Western Art*, Vol. II (Acts of the Twentieth International Congress of the History of Art). Princeton, 1963.

Lotz, W. "Notizen zum Kirchlichen Zentralbau der Renaissance," *Studien zur toskanischen Kunst* Festschrift für L. H. Heydenreich. Munich, 1964.

Forster, K. W. "From 'Rocca' to 'Civitas': Urban planning at Sabbioneta," *L'Arte*, fasc. 5, March, 1969.

# INDEX

# SOURCES OF ILLUSTRATIONS

Aerofilms, London: 81

Alinari, Florence: 34, 35, 40, 43, 46

Anderson, Florence: 32, 47

Giulio C. Argan: 4, 11, 17, 18, 26, 49, 51, 55, 58, 65, 67, 68, 69, 70, 71, 75, 76, 86, 89, 90, 103

Braun and Hogenberg, *Civitates Orbis Terrarum:* 83, 85, 96, 97, 99

*Codice Magliabechiano del Trattato di Francesco di Giorgio Martini:* 6, 7, 8, 9

De Fer, *Les Forces de l'Europe ou descriptions des principaux villes avec leurs fortifications:* 82, 84, 88, 92, 94, 98, 102, 104

Filarete, *Il Codia dell'architettura:* 5

Foto Borlui: 77

Foto ENIT: 1, 13, 14, 15, 20, 21, 22, 29, 33, 36, 37, 41, 42, 44, 45, 52, 57, 59, 63, 64, 73, 74

Foto Pellegrini: 2

Fotocielo, Rome: 16, 23, 53, 54, 66, 101

Fotomero, Urbino: 19

Gallerie Gabinetto Fotografico, Florence: 38

Galleria Nazionale delle Marche, Urbino: 25

Morini: 10

Private Collection, Rome: 56

A. Sciaro, *I monumenti di Pienza,* 1942: 24

Sebastiano Serlio, *Tutte l'opere d'architettura:* 28

Courtesy of Soprintendenza alle Gallerie dei Firenze: 39

Courtesy of Soprintendenza alle Galleria di Mantova: 78, 79

Staatliche Museum, Berlin: 26

*Theatrum Urbium Italicarum* by Pietro Bertelli: 30, 31, 48, 72, 80, 91, 95, 98, 100, 105

*Trattato di Daniel Speckle:* 12

Uffizi Gallery, Florence: 27

Bruno Zevi: 50

Bruno Zevi and Paolo Portoghesi, eds., *Michelangiolo architetto:* 60, 61, 62